Life During the American Revolution

D1604511

The Way People Live

Life During the American Revolution

Titles in The Way People Live series include:

THE WAY PEOPLE LIVE

Life During the American Revolution

by
Stuart A. Kallen

LUCENT BOOKS
SAN DIEGO, CALIFORNIA

THOMSON

GALE

Detroit • New York • San Diego • San Francisco
Boston • New Haven, Conn. • Waterville, Maine
London • Munich

On cover: Engraving of a colonial kitchen.

Library of Congress Cataloging-in-Publication Data

Kallen, Stuart A., 1955–
    Life during the American Revolution / by Stuart A. Kallen.
        p. cm. — (The way people live)
    Includes bibliographical references and index.
        ISBN 1-59018-007-0 (hardback : alk. paper)
    1. United States—History—Revolution, 1775–1783—Social aspects—Juvenile
literature. 2. United States—Social conditions—To 1865—Juvenile literature.
3. United States—Social life and customs—1775–1783—Juvenile literature.
4. Soldiers—United States—Social conditions—18th century—Juvenile literature.
5. Women—United States—Social conditions—18th century—Juvenile literature. 6. African Americans—Social conditions—18th century—Juvenile literature. 7. Indians of North America—Social conditions—18th century—Juvenile
literature. [1. United States—History—Revolution, 1775–1783. 2. United
States—Social conditions—To 1865. 3. United States—Social life and customs—
1775–1783. 4. Soldiers—Social conditions—18th century. 5. Women—Social
conditions—18th century. 6. African Americans—Social conditions—18th century. 7. Indians of North America—Social conditions—18th century.] I. Title.
II. Series.
    E209 .K34 2002
    973.3'1—dc21

                                                                    2001005249

Copyright 2002 by Lucent Books,
an imprint of The Gale Group
10911 Technology Place, San Diego, California 92127

Printed in the U.S.A.

Contents

Discovering the Humanity in Us All

Books in The Way People Live series focus on groups of people in a wide variety of circumstances, settings, and time periods. Some books focus on different cultural groups, others, on people in a particular historical time period, while others cover people involved in a specific event. Each book emphasizes the daily routines, personal and historical struggles, and achievements of people from all walks of life.

To really understand any culture, it is necessary to strip the mind of the common notions we hold about groups of people. These stereotypes are the archenemies of learning. It does not even matter whether the stereotypes are positive or negative; they are confining and tight. Removing them is a challenge that's not easily met, as anyone who has ever tried it will admit. Ideas that do not fit into the templates we create are unwelcome visitors—ones we would prefer remain quietly in a corner or forgotten room.

The cowboy of the Old West is a good example of such confining roles. The cowboy was courageous, yet soft-spoken. His time (it is always a he, in our template) was spent alternatively saving a rancher's daughter from certain death on a runaway stagecoach, or shooting it out with rustlers. At times, of course, he was likely to get a little crazy in town after a trail drive, but for the most part, he was the epitome of inner strength. It is disconcerting to find out that the cowboy is human, even a bit childish. Can it really be true that cowboys would line up to help the cook on the trail drive grind coffee, just hoping he would give them a little stick of peppermint candy that came with the coffee shipment? The idea of tough cowboys vying with one another to help "Coosie" (as they called their cooks) for a bit of candy seems silly and out of place.

So is the vision of Eskimos playing video games and watching MTV, living in prefab housing in the Arctic. It just does not fit with what "Eskimo" means. We are far more comfortable with snow igloos and whale blubber, harpoons and kayaks.

Although the cultures dealt with in Lucent's The Way People Live series are often historically and socially well known, the emphasis is on the personal aspects of life. Groups of people, while unquestionably affected by their politics and their governmental structures, are more than those institutions. How do people in a particular time and place educate their children? What do they eat? And how do they build their houses? What kinds of work do they do? What kinds of games do they enjoy? The answers to these questions bring these cultures to life. People's lives are revealed in the particulars and only by knowing the particulars can we understand these cultures' will to survive and their moments of weakness and greatness.

This is not to say that understanding politics does not help to understand a culture. There is no question that the Warsaw ghetto, for example, was a culture that was brought about by the politics and social ideas of Adolf

Hitler and the Third Reich. But the Jews who were crowded together in the ghetto cannot be understood by the Reich's politics. Their life was a day-to-day battle for existence, and the creativity and methods they used to prolong their lives is a vital story of human perseverance that would be denied by focusing only on the institutions of Hitler's Germany. Knowing that children as young as five or six outwitted Nazi guards on a daily basis, that Jewish policemen helped the Germans control the ghetto, that children attended secret schools in the ghetto and even earned diplomas—these are the things that reveal the fabric of life, that can inspire, intrigue, and amaze.

Books in The Way People Live series allow both the casual reader and the student to see humans as victims, heroes, and onlookers. And although humans act in ways that can fill us with feelings of sorrow and revulsion, it is important to remember that "hero," "predator," and "victim" are dangerous terms. Heaping undue pity or praise on people reduces them to objects, and strips them of their humanity.

Seeing the Jews of Warsaw only as victims is to deny their humanity. Seeing them only as they appear in surviving photos, staring at the camera with infinite sadness, is limiting, both to them and to those who want to understand them. To an object of pity the only appropriate response becomes "Those poor creatures!" and that reduces both the quality of their struggle and the depth of their despair. No one is served by such two-dimensional views of people and their cultures.

With this in mind, The Way People Live series strives to flesh out the traditional, two-dimensional views of people in various cultures and historical circumstances. Using a wide variety of primary quotations—the words not only of the politicians and government leaders, but of the real people whose lives are being examined—each book in the series attempts to show an honest and complete picture of a culture removed from our own by time or space.

By examining cultures in this way, the reader will notice not only the glaring differences from his or her own culture, but also will be struck by the similarities. For indeed, people share common needs—warmth, good company, stability, and affirmation from others. Ultimately, seeing how people really live, or have lived, can only enrich our understanding of ourselves.

Seeds of Revolution

From the time the first European settlers landed on the East Coast in the early 1600s, they began to reshape the North American continent to suit their needs. They cut down forests for lumber, drained wetlands to plant crops, diverted streams to power mills, and built little cities in the wilderness that often resembled the European villages they had left behind.

The Native Americans who had inhabited the land for tens of thousands of years were either pushed off their land, killed by disease, or slaughtered. The priceless natural resources that they had regarded with reverence and respect were cut down, dug up, surveyed, and sold. The lumber, minerals, and animal furs not used by the exploding population of white colonists were loaded on ships and offered for sale in France, Spain, the Netherlands, Great Britain, and elsewhere.

The land that was once home to the Lenape, the Wampanoag, the Penobscot, the Cherokee, and other Native American tribes was fought over by the most powerful nations in

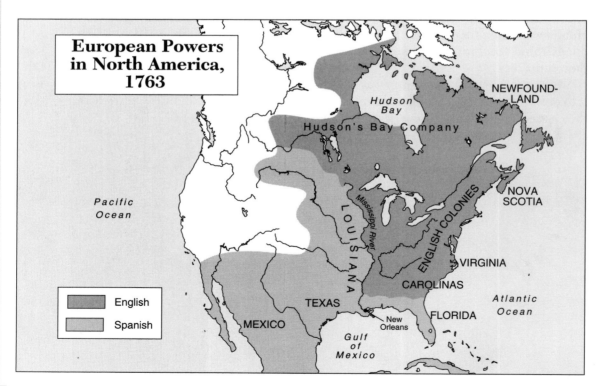

European Powers in North America, 1763

Pacific Ocean

Hudson Bay

Hudson's Bay Company

NEWFOUND-LAND

NOVA SCOTIA

LOUISIANA

Mississippi River

ENGLISH COLONIES

VIRGINIA

CAROLINAS

Atlantic Ocean

TEXAS

MEXICO

New Orleans

FLORIDA

Gulf of Mexico

English

Spanish

Europe. By the eighteenth century Great Britain governed much of the East Coast, while France controlled the Great Lakes region and Canada. The first Americans who had managed to survive were scattered, moving east to Ohio, Wisconsin, Michigan, and elsewhere to escape white civilization. Others lived a precarious existence near colonial towns and villages.

War and Taxes

In 1754 the French and Indian War broke out between Great Britain and France. Americans in the thirteen colonies were loyal to Britain and helped defeat the French and their Native American allies in 1763. After the war, the British Empire controlled all of the land in North America from the East Coast to the Mississippi River, and from Canada down to Florida, which was claimed by Spain.

However the cost of the war had nearly bankrupted the British treasury and nearly doubled the British national debt. Britain's ruling body, called Parliament, felt that the Americans should help pay for the war since the colonists had gained a great deal of security when the French were evicted.

In addition the British wanted to control the labor and goods produced by the 2 million American colonists. This policy is explained on a website maintained by the Indian King Tavern Museum in Haddonfield, New Jersey:

> The very structure of colonial empire was designed to maintain its inhabitants in economic servitude. Colonial business was supposed to produce low-cost raw materials that were shipped exclusively to England to be turned into finished, high-profit goods by British factories and mills. Strict laws prohibited colonists from establishing inland settlements beyond the reach of royal governors; iron works . . . were only allowed to produce ingots of iron, not finished metal products. It was illegal for colonial tradesmen to export even such common products as hats; many tradesmen were restricted by law from having more than two apprentices to prevent them from establishing factory-like production operations.[1]

To maintain strict control over Americans and their business endeavors, the British rulers passed a series of laws intended to raise taxes in order to pay off the war debt. The Sugar Act of 1764 placed import duties on sugar and molasses brought in from the West Indies. The Stamp Act of 1765 required colonists to purchase tax stamps to be affixed to all newspapers, pamphlets, legal documents, and even playing cards and dice.

A tax stamp, one source of American hostility toward Britain.

Since the colonists had no representatives in the British Parliament, they bitterly protested these taxes, claiming they should not be forced into taxation without representation. And while this law may have seemed like a good idea to members of Parliament, it outraged lawyers, businessmen, newspaper editors, and journalists who were forced to purchase the stamps. These were the very people with the intelligence, wealth, and power needed to raise widespread protest against the Stamp Act.

Protests and a Tea Party

Although the Stamp Act was repealed in 1766, another law enacted in 1767, the Townshend Act, placed import duties on glass, paint, paper, and the favorite drink of the colonists, tea. To protest the tea tax, a secret organization known as the Sons of Liberty was formed in towns throughout America. Colonists began a boycott of British goods and began a program to prevent importation of European goods. By the end of 1769 all of the colonies except New Hampshire had passed nonimportation legislation.

In response the British government ordered thousands of red-coated soldiers to America to keep protesters in line. At a rowdy street demonstration in Boston in 1770, the crowd provoked the redcoats, or "lobster backs," to fire on the demonstrators. Five men were killed, including Crispus Attucks, an African American protester.

Three years later, continued anger over the tea tax resulted in the Boston Tea Party, in which about 150 men disguised as Native Americans threw $1 million worth of British tea into the Boston Harbor. By April 1775, the first shots in the Revolutionary War were fired in Lexington and Concord, Massachusetts.

A Deeply Divided Country

In 1776 Thomas Paine published a pamphlet called *Common Sense* in which he urged Americans to separate from England. In it he wrote,

Ye that oppose independence now, ye know not what ye do; ye are opening a door to eternal tyranny. . . . There are thousands, and tens of thousands, who would think it glorious to expel from the continent, that barbarous and hellish power [of Great Britain].[2]

Thomas Paine's Common Sense *was a runaway best-seller in its time.*

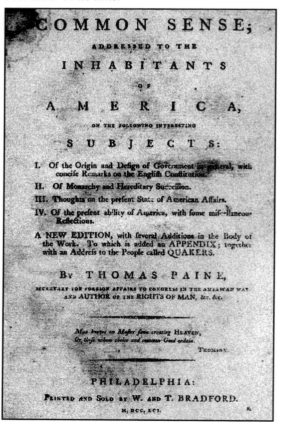

Paine's tract sold more than one hundred thousand copies within three months, setting a publishing record that would stand for more than two centuries. Up and down the East Coast, average citizens who read *Common Sense* began to take sides in the conflict. In July, delegates from all thirteen colonies signed the Declaration of Independence, and George Washington was appointed to form an army to fight Great Britain—the most powerful nation on earth.

A political cartoon of the time urges the colonies to unite against Great Britain.

As the colonies committed themselves to war, only about one-third of Americans openly supported the Revolution; these were known as patriots. An equal number, called loyalists, remained devoted to Great Britain. The rest refused to take sides, unwilling to risk their property and their lives. The opinions of the Native Americans, free blacks, and slaves were rarely taken into account by the powerful men who were leading the nation to war.

Meanwhile the loyalties of neighbors, friends, and family members were deeply divided. Even Benjamin Franklin, one of the most outspoken supporters of revolution, found division within his family. His son William, the governor of New Jersey, remained loyal to the British even though he was imprisoned and tortured.

As the war escalated, those who supported independence formed roving gangs that traveled the countryside pillaging and burning farms of loyalists. State governments passed laws to confiscate the property of those who supported Great Britain. And people were whipped, tarred and feathered, and hanged if they were suspected of siding with the loyalists.

About one hundred thousand people left the colonies altogether, fleeing to Canada or England. About thirty to fifty thousand joined the British to fight their revolutionary neighbors. In the South slaves were promised their freedom if they joined the English army. In the North, blacks fought with the Continental Army.

The war was fought in the countryside, in the western frontier, and in the cities. Some of the bloodiest battles were waged near New York City. Later the English army seized Philadelphia, the second largest city in the British Empire. And so it continued for six long years. As in most wars, women, children, and the elderly faced especially terrible hardships.

Despite the deprivations and suffering, it was common Americans who fought and won the Revolution, as Ray Raphael writes in *A People's History of the American Revolution:*

Common people functioned as key operatives at all stages [of the Revolution]: they started the war, they ran the committees, they fought the battles. Laborers and seamen dumped tea into the Boston harbor. Thousands of nameless farmers closed the courts in Massachusetts, terminating British rule. Crowds gathered anywhere and everywhere, armed with buckets of tar and baskets of feathers to enforce revolutionaries' standards [upon those who opposed them].[3]

Farm and Village Life

Colonial America during the Revolution was a mostly rural place. More than 85 percent of all citizens lived in the country, farming the land to support themselves. There were some towns and villages scattered throughout the countryside, but these were very small, none home to more than two or three thousand inhabitants.

Although rural people were isolated from larger cities such as Boston, New York, and Philadelphia, they were well aware of events that led to the American Revolution. Beginning with the Stamp Act in 1765, heated political discussions over taxes, loyalties, and impending war occupied the farmers, craftsmen, and merchants who lived in rural areas. News traveled very slowly, however, so the demands of King George and the colonial protesters were largely distant rumblings for most farm families, who labored from sunup to sundown to ensure their survival.

The Rural Scene

In the early 1770s, as the Revolutionary War loomed, a person passing through the New England countryside would have first noticed

A summer scene on a small, prosperous farm in New York.

Bad Roads: A Joking Matter

In the 1770s, the rutted trails in New England were so bad that locals joked that a man could be swallowed up by the deep mud. In *The Embattled Farmers*, Nathaniel Newcomer relates a joke that was passed around when the roads turned into virtual swamps.

"In the [early] era of American transportation a stock tale circulated throughout the country districts every year about the time of the spring rains. It concerned a local character who on surveying a particularly muddy portion of the village street spied a man's broad-brimmed hat lying there. Gingerly feeling his way out into the quagmire, he picked up the hat and found, much to his surprise, a man's head underneath. 'Oh, I don't need any help,' the man said, 'I've got a good horse under me, and I can feel that he's just struck solid ground.'"

muddy, rutted roads. As Nathaniel Newcomer writes in *The Embattled Farmers,*

[Poor] roads usually formed the traveler's first and most lasting impression of the countryside. Not only were the roads bad . . . but in many cases they were little more than bridle paths cut through the forests, hollowed out into ravines or gullies by the rains and unimproved except by clearing and the construction of a few rude bridges. Routes were not well marked, and [in] even the most settled areas a wayfarer might get [in the terms of the day] "most Confoundedly Lost."[4]

Although the roads were rough, they were dotted with charming farmhouses and barns perched on the edges of streams, lakes, and rivers. The average farm was less than one hundred acres, and fields were planted with oats, flax, potatoes, hay, corn, and wheat. Behind the small farmsteads, apple, cherry, peach, pear, and plum trees adorned small clearings on forested hillsides. Pastures were divided by split-rail fences and miles of fieldstone walls.

The planting methods of the Revolutionary era farmer had changed little since the Middle Ages. In spring, the yeoman used two to six oxen to pull his wooden plow across the hard, rocky soil. The blade of the plow was coated with sheet iron or old saw blades and tipped with brittle iron that often broke, putting an end to the day's labors.

Grain was simply sowed by broadcasting —that is, throwing the seeds over a wide area by hand. Weeds were chopped from the ground with a hoe or pulled by hand, and the finished product was cut with a scythe. The grain was hauled to the barn in two-wheel carts or crude barrows. Kernels of grain were separated from hulls by a manual threshing device with a long wooden handle and free-swinging stick attached to its end called a flail. Farmers made the wooden parts of their tools during the cold winter months; the metal parts were supplied by local blacksmiths.

Nearly all New England farmers owned their own land, and huge tracts of land were simply there for the taking, as Oscar and Lilian Handlin write in *A Restless People:*

Land was abundant. Whoever wished to work could build a home and put a plow to the soil. If the price of the desired acres was high in the eastern counties, it was low in the western; let the seeker go

A replica of an eighteenth-century New Hampshire farmhouse. Farmers adopted the food crops of the Native Americans and imitated their cultivation techniques, due to the extremely rocky soil in the area.

but far enough and he would find a place in the woods, his for the taking. To those who measured by the standards of crowded European holdings, America was abundant almost beyond belief. Not land but labor was in short supply.[5]

Most farmers raised the crops they needed and often had extra to sell at weekly markets. Their agricultural products, such as flaxseed, corn, cattle, and horses, were also in great demand in coastal cities, and were exported to the West Indies and Europe. Though some achieved great wealth this way, there were few ostentatious displays of affluence. Most houses had fewer than six or seven rooms and were filled with simple, functional furniture. As one author wrote in 1775, "In New England . . . the little freeholders [estate owners] and farmers live in the midst of a plenty of all the necessaries of life; they do not acquire wealth, but they have comforts of abundance."[6]

The Farm Family's Life

Although most farms were run by families, some people owned larger landholdings and rented them to tenant farmers, or used Native Americans, black slaves, or white servants to do the work. In New England, however, unlike in the South, slavery and indentured servitude were rare by the 1770s.

Farmers occasionally employed masons, carpenters, housepainters, and field hands to help them when necessary. There were a few skilled trade workers in the small villages that dotted the countryside. During the long New England winters, however, members of farm families often drew on their own talents to produce goods for monetary gain. Farmers doubled as shoemakers, harness makers, metalworkers, coopers (barrel makers), broom makers, wine and cider makers, beer brewers, vinegar distillers, lumbermen, furniture makers, textile workers, pottery makers, glassblowers, surveyors, millers, and so on.

The extra money, according to the Handlins, was used for "paying taxes and dues to the church and [for] making occasional purchases—of guns or powder, of pots, axes, saws, salt, rum, and other goods [the farmer] could not himself fabricate."[7]

Demand for products crafted by farmers was high, as the population of New England grew at the speedy pace of about 2 percent a year. With such a rapid influx of people, most of the best land was taken by the early eighteenth century. Newcomers were often forced to practice subsistence agriculture in the rocky hills found on the western frontiers of New England. The first step was to build a house as quickly as possible, as Patrick M'Robert wrote in 1774 in *A Tour Through Part of the North Provinces of America:*

The houses in the back settlements are generally all built of logs at first, which when [settlers] take pains to square and lay right, make very good houses for many years: but the new settlers are generally in such a hurry to get up their houses, that they pile up round trees one above another, notching them at the corners to hinder them from falling, saw out a door and windows, and bind a roof, covering it with bark instead of shingles, and plaistering up the joints between the trees with clay and straw: with these they put up for some years, till they find leisure and ability to build better.[8]

Since the newcomers did not have land that was suitable for cattle, fruits, or other produce, they adopted the food crops of the Native Americans and imitated their cultivation techniques. Corn, beans, and squash, for instance, were planted together in mounds about three feet tall and five feet across.

Simple tools such as pitchforks, spades, and axes were essential to farming in America in the late 1700s.

The Farmer's Hardships

Although life might have been secure for New England farmers in the 1770s, it was by no means easy, as Oscar and Lilian Handlin explain in *A Restless People*.

"Neither soil nor climate was congenial to a life of leisure. Harsh winters, relatively short growing seasons, and unpredictable weather demanded constant vigilance. Once the husbandmen [farmers] had stripped the forests away, they discovered the deficiencies of the land. And since only hard labor could win a livelihood from the earth, most farmland remained unimproved. No matter how extensive his holdings on paper, a man alone could manage to cultivate only three or four acres. In the absence of sons or servants it was more prudent to devote large tracts to meadows or woodlots, for it was easy to raise livestock so long as one let the beasts feed and breed as they would. Hence, too, the preference in the region for corn, which kept better than wheat, required relatively little labor, and left stalk leaves and husks to feed the animals.

Families content to live on pickled pork and clothe themselves in plain home-spun textiles tolerated the indolence of adults and the idleness of children. But anyone who wished to do more than barely hold on worked hard to hoe the vegetable garden, gather nuts, and tend the poultry and the apple trees.

The unending struggle shaped Yankee character. The lesson that life was a battle against uncongenial elements, learned early in life, trained people to strive lest they go under. The failures plunged into poverty, a sign of personal defeat that brought with it the additional degradation of relief from public charity, or open auction for support by the best bidder. The old and the disabled as well as widows and orphans fared badly in rural New England, dependent as they were for aid on relatives with limited means, or on towns which resented every charge that increased taxes in a society always short of funds."

When the corn was planted, a dead fish was buried next to it to fertilize the plant.

The corn grew tall by late July. The bean vines wrapped themselves around the corn stalks, and the squash and gourds covered the ground and prevented weeds from sprouting. And, as M'Robert writes, "They often sow some melon [or] cucumber along with the Indian corn, which soon grows to perfection in the open fields."[9]

With this simple farming method, subsistence farmers needed few tools, relying on hoes, digging sticks, saws, and axes to survive. They augmented their diets with their muskets, hunting squirrels, rabbits, wild turkeys, ducks, and other game.

Villages and Politics

In addition to the farms on the western frontier of civilization, dozens of small villages were scattered throughout the New England countryside. Most people lived within seven or eight miles of a village like the one described by Newcomer:

There, grouped irregularly around the town common and the Congregational church were found the crossroads store, the tavern, the artisan's shop, the tiny schoolhouse, and perhaps half a hundred chimneyed homes. But houses were generally an unpainted, weathered gray, streets were not always trim and neat. . . .

Occasionally [travelers would stop] at the beckoning tavern to drink a cheering mug of rum or [a beer and rum cocktail called a] "West India Flip," and perhaps to watch [a black entertainer] fiddle and dance to amuse the paying customers. The patrons at the bar would be mostly farmers and possibly an itinerant peddler or a merchant on his way to Boston. . . . Conversation, of course, would revolve around the weather and crop conditions.[10]

Taverns also served as meetinghouses and informal post offices. And although newspapers were not in great supply, single copies of the *Boston Gazette* and other papers were often brought by messengers on horseback to rural villages and posted on the walls of local taverns.

From the time of the Stamp Act in 1765, these papers informed local farmers about

the red-hot revolutionary tensions between the British government, colonial assemblies, and political agitators in the streets. And many farmers considered themselves experts on such issues, prompting British loyalist Ann Hulton to write in *Letters of a Loyalist Lady,* "They are all politicians."[11]

Though Hulton's comment was meant to be derisive, the people of Massachusetts did experience a high level of political engagement. Any male could vote as long as he was over the age of twenty-one, had lived in a town for more than a year, and owned property equal to the month's wages of a laborer. In many villages this meant that seven out of ten men were engaged in political activities, including running for office. Even though women, blacks, Native Americans, and the very poor were kept from voting, the Massachusetts voting laws were some of the most liberal in the country. But, as in modern times, politics were often bitter and divisive.

For example, when the Townshend Act imposed taxes on tea in 1767, stubborn New

Newspapers such as the Massachusetts Sun *kept rural settlements informed about the events taking place in the cities.*

Englanders enacted the "nonimportation" movement, refusing to buy any imported goods from England, including tea. Many rural merchants—especially those who supported Great Britain—continued to sell tea and other banned goods. Those who supported the boycott raided loyalist stores at midnight and confiscated imported goods. A few shops were put to the torch. More important, a propaganda war was waged in print, with handbills that read, while "an Indian drinks cyder . . . an importer drinks the blood of his countrymen."[12]

In 1772, the Sons of Liberty began committees of correspondence to communicate with farmers and rural residents and keep them informed of the hostilities. In return the farmers drew up their own anti-British tracts. For example, the farmers of Petersham, Massachusetts, signed a petition that blamed the British of "Draining the People of the Fruits of their Toil."[13]

Tea, Tar, and Feathers

After the Boston Tea Party in late 1773 the British enacted the Boston Port Bill, also known as the first of the "Coercive Acts." This measure prevented merchants from exporting their goods from Boston Harbor. In addition to destroying the colonial economy in Boston, the act also affected farmers who depended on grain exports to earn a living. As a result of the Port Bill most New England farmers united in support of the patriot cause.

In protest the patriots stepped up the enforcement of the tea boycott, and committees of correspondence became "committees of correspondence and inspection." Rural residents of Brimfield, Massachusetts, began to "inspect Tea Drinkers, and if they shall know or find out any Person who shall still continue to Use, Sell, or Consume in their families any East India Tea, to post up their names in some public place, that they may be known and Despised."[14]

As the rhetoric sharpened, rural families who did not support the patriot cause found themselves outcasts. Merchants would refuse to barter with them, and neighbors no longer came to visit. Those who held a grudge or wanted to destroy a neighbor's reputation needed only to falsely accuse them of drinking the forbidden tea.

When public ostracism failed to sway a loyalist, patriots sometimes turned to violence. Those who supported the British might have their stores burned or their fields and crops destroyed. Others were tortured until they signed oaths swearing allegiance to the patriot cause. For example, Israel Williams, a merchant in the village of Hatfield, Massachusetts, was locked in a cabin with his son after patriots started a fire in a fireplace that was plugged from the outside. After several hours choking in the unbearable smoke, the Williamses finally signed the oath.

Then there were those who endured the living torture of being tarred and feathered. People subjected to this treatment were held down while foul-smelling, boiling-hot tar and pillow feathers were poured over their bodies. Raphael printed instructions for this torturous treatment from an unnamed source:

First, strip a Person naked, then heat the Tar untill it is thin, & pour it upon the naked Flesh, or rub it over with a Tar Brush. . . . After which, sprinkle decently upon the Tar, whilst it is yet warm, as many Feathers as will stick to it. Then hold a lighted Candle to the Feathers, & try to set it all on Fire; if it will burn so much the better. But as the Experiment is often made in cold Weather; it will not then suc-

> # WILLIAM JACKSON,
>
> an *IMPORTER*; at the
>
> # BRAZEN HEAD,
>
> *North Side of the* TOWN-HOUSE,
>
> and *Oppofite the Town-Pump, in*
>
> *Corn-hill,* B O S T O N.
>
> It is defired that the SONS and
> DAUGHTERS of *LIBERTY*,
> would not buy any one thing of
> him, for in fo doing they will bring
> Difgrace upon *themfelves*, and their
> *Pofterity*, for *ever* and *ever*, AMEN.

The Sons and Daughters of Liberty posted broadsides in taverns urging citizens to boycott merchants who were loyal to the British government.

ceed—take also an Halter & put it round the Person's Neck, & then cart him the Rounds [and threaten him with hanging].[15]

Removal of the cooled tar was equally painful. Entire strips of skin came off, and the wounds often became infected. Some died from the shock, while others went insane. After being tarred and feathered, the burned and terrorized loyalist might be carried away tied to a fence rail while his property was confiscated by the colonial government. Having been "run out of town on a rail," some fled to big cities or back to Great Britain; others went to Canada or Spanish-controlled Florida.

Although only a handful of loyalists were ever given this ghastly punishment their humiliations became legend in rural areas. For example, one loyalist was forced to march twenty miles with a live goose under his arm. Then he was made to pluck the feathers for his own tarring and thank the crowd for the treatment, after which he was driven out of town to the din of beating drums. In East Haddam, Connecticut, farmer Abner Beebe was treated to a hog-dung-and-feathers party. Although not as painful as being tarred and feathered, being coated in pig manure was extremely mortifying for the well-to-do loyalist farmer.

Patriotism and Liberty Poles

Patriot leaders had other, more positive methods for rallying support for their cause.

Farm and Village Life

In many rural villages tall wooden shafts called liberty poles were erected in town squares to remind people of the patriot cause. On the eve of the Revolutionary War villages had contests to see who could erect the tallest liberty pole, and some topped over 135 feet. The value of the symbol was stated by an unnamed Son of Liberty, who said that the pole "Strikes the eye of the Beholder even at a Distance and in the most natural easy and ready manner puts him in mind of his Liberty and rights."[16]

Liberty poles were erected in village squares amid much drinking and merrymaking.

The minuteman was expected to supply himself with a good weapon, gunpowder, and a knapsack, and to be ready for war at a moment's notice.

The poles also served as meeting places where patriots would gather to eat, drink liquor, and make speeches. Leaders also recognized the power of music to unite people, and songs were an integral part of political rallies. Among rural residents "Yankee Doodle" was sung regularly, with dozens of verses celebrating battle and satirizing the soldier's life.

Forming Militias

By 1774 patriotic speeches had turned to preparations for war. In small towns and villages across the countryside, government officials began raising money to train militias and buy arms and ammunition. All able-bodied men between the ages of sixteen and fifty were signed into "training bands" to learn the ways of the military. Those up to age seventy were put on the "alarm list" to be called in an emergency. Men in the training band were ex-pected to be ready for war at a moment's notice, so they adopted the name "minutemen." Each man was expected to supply himself with a good weapon, gunpowder, and a knapsack.

On Saturday afternoons these ragtag soldiers assembled for training in town squares throughout New England. Deserters from the British army might be hired to train the men, and the patriotic spirit was increased with plenty of free beer. Local women and children would gather to watch the spectacle. The day would end with patriotic speeches as the crowd roared. With passions thus inflamed, the will of the people was cemented, and the self-reliant New England villagers were ready for war.

The Tobacco Coast

It is the great paradox of the American Revolution that the democratic, egalitarian, and independence-loving farmers of New England found their greatest allies in the Virginia colony. For it was there on the Chesapeake Bay —known as the Tobacco Coast—that wealthy aristocrats used slave laborers to produce addictive tobacco products, for which they were rewarded with great riches. In fact, some of the most famous founding fathers, such as George Washington and Thomas Jefferson, who today are remembered as great statesmen were, first and foremost, tobacco planters.

The first tobacco grown in the Chesapeake region was planted by John Rolfe in 1612. By the eighteenth century a large majority of American and European men—and some women—were addicted to the leafy weed. Originally grown by Native Americans and smoked to offer prayer and attract spirits, tobacco was believed to be a wonder drug by eighteenth-century colonists. They used it as medicine for headaches, bruises, toothaches, and even congested lungs. It was powdered and sniffed up the nose to clear the mind, smoked in pipes and cigars, and chewed.

Although the promise of tobacco offered riches, it was a difficult crop to grow; a single farmer could only cultivate about three to five acres per year. After the tobacco was planted in mounds about four to six feet apart, someone had to handpick large white caterpillars called tobacco cutworms from the plant and crush them between the fingers. This job was most often accomplished by slaves or small children.

A farmer could expect to harvest about five hundred pounds of tobacco per acre of land. At the end of the season, the leaves were picked in the field and the plants were

Slaves provided the labor at tobacco farms such as this one on the Chesapeake Bay.

The Planter's Life

With slaves and servants doing all the work, wealthy tobacco farmers had little to do all day. In 1784, John Ferdinand Dalziel Smyth described a typical day of a wealthy southern planter in volume 1 of *A Tour in the United States of America.*

"The gentleman of fortune rises about nine o'clock; he perhaps may make an excursion to walk as far as his stables to see his horses, which is seldom more than fifty yards from his house; he returns to breakfast, between nine and ten, which is generally tea or coffee, bread and butter, and very thin slices of venison, or hung beef. He then lies down on a pallet, and the floor, and the coolest room with [in] the house, in his shirt and trousers only, with a negro at his head, and another at his feet, to fan him, and keep off the flies; between twelve and one he takes a draft of bombo, or toddy, a liquor composed of water, sugar, rum, and nutmeg, which is made weak, and kept cool: he dances between two and three, and at every table, of whatever else there may be, a ham and greens or cabbage, is always a standing dish; at dinner he drinks cyder, toddy, punch, port, claret, and madeira, which is generally excellent here: after dinner he returns to his pallet, with two blacks to fan him, and continues to drink toddy . . . all the afternoon. . . . Between nine and ten in the evening, he eats a light supper of milk and fruit, or wine, sugar, and fruit &tc. and almost immediately retires to bed for the night; in which, if it not be furnished with musketoe [mosquito] curtains, he is generally so molested with the heat, and harassed and tormented with those pernicious insects the musketoes, that [it is impossible to] sleep."

hung on poles and carried to the drying barn by two people who balanced the load on their shoulders. After curing for several days the tobacco was packed into large barrels called hogsheads, weighing up to nine hundred pounds apiece.

Farmers might make several thousand dollars from their yearly crop—enough to live comfortably—but tobacco was very hard on the soil. As Daniel J. Boorstin writes in *The Americans: the Colonial Experience,*

Since [the tobacco farmers] did not replenish the nitrogen and potash which growing tobacco sucked from the soil, it was only on virgin land that tobacco could flourish; the second crop was usually the best. After the fourth season land was customarily abandoned to corn and wheat, before finally being turned back to wild pine, sorrel, and sedge. Under this system a prudent planter dared not put more than a small portion—say, ten percent—of his acreage in tobacco at any one time.[17]

As a result tobacco farmers were forced to continually cut trees, burn the underbrush, pull up the stumps, and clear new lands to keep their crop in production.

Many owners of small farms in the region depended as much on hunting for survival as they did on their tobacco crops. As soon as young men were old enough to handle a gun, they went out looking for birds and small animals. As the Handlins write, "The great quantities of game made them excellent marksmen, and thousands supported their families in this way. Where deer and turkey were abundant

George Washington's plantation at Mount Vernon, Virginia, could not have operated without free slave labor.

for the shooting, the plow offered few attractions."[18] When the Revolution broke out, these skilled marksmen were often able to inflict a great number of casualties upon the enemy using techniques they had developed hunting in the backwoods.

The "Tobacco Aristocracy"

The lives of the people in the Virginia colony were completely centered around tobacco. As T.H. Breen writes in *Tobacco Culture,*

> Tobacco touched nearly every aspect of their existence. It was a source of the colony's prosperity, a medium for commercial transactions and payment of local taxes, and a theme of decorative art. Indeed, the majority of the planters' waking hours were spent, as they would have said, in "making a crop." Almost every surviving . . . book from this period

contains a detailed description of tobacco production.[19]

And no one was more preoccupied by tobacco than the 10 percent of planters around the Chesapeake Bay who were known as the "Tobacco Aristocracy."

To the poor farmers around them the Tobacco Aristocracy seemed to be obsessed with obtaining wealth, constructing huge mansions, importing luxurious material goods from Europe, and maintaining large crews of slaves. These men often inspired a mix of awe and fear among the common people. In the 1760s a young man named James Ireland, who had little in the way of material wealth, described a wealthy Virginia planter riding down the road: "When I viewed him riding up . . . I never beheld such display of pride in any man . . . arising from his deportment, attitude and gesture; he rode a lofty elegant horse. . . . His countenance appeared to me as bold and daring as satan [*sic*] himself."[20]

George Washington was part of the tobacco aristocracy. The commander of the Continental Army owned about 275 slaves at the time of the Revolution. Mark Mastromarino describes Washington's life in rural Virginia on the eve of the Revolution on the Papers of George Washington website:

[Gentlemen] like Washington [displayed] their social status by maintaining a lavish lifestyle modeled after that of the British landed gentry and aristocracy. Washington especially enjoyed the displays this entailed, such as renovating his mansion in the latest style and filling it with the finest furnishings, stocking his cellars with vintage Madeira [wine], acquiring the best-blooded horses for his stables, keeping a deer park and riding to the hounds, conducting agricultural experiments, extending expansive hospitality to neighbors and strangers, and sacrificing some of his leisure time to serve in public office.[21]

Tobacco and Revolution

Every year after harvest Washington and the other Virginia planters loaded the bulk of their tobacco on ships bound for England, where agents sold it for the best price possible. As a result the settled, well-to-do planters had extremely close ties to Great Britain and, as late as the 1760s, had no intention of fomenting revolution. The unpredictable economics of tobacco, however, pushed them toward the independence movement.

Planters large and small found themselves forever in debt to corrupt British export agents who charged growers exorbitant sums for freight and transportation to European markets. This heavy debt was extremely burdensome to the proud planters, as Breen

George Washington himself was a member of the "Tobacco Aristocracy."

writes: "John Mercer, an old man nearly driven to distraction by the accumulating weight of debt, told his son in 1768 that he would welcome death were he not responsible for the welfare of his wife and children."[22]

By this time, tobacco farmers owed millions of pounds to the mercantile houses that handled tobacco transactions. As such, tobacco would play an important part in the Revolution—so much so that the people in the Chesapeake Bay region called the Revolutionary War the "Tobacco War." Many planters believed that nothing short of American independence would free them from the clutches of the corrupt tobacco wholesalers.

When the bottom dropped out of the tobacco market in 1772, bankruptcy swept through the countryside. Many Virginia planters felt they had little choice but to join the movement toward independence.

Effects of Revolution

By April 1775 the "shots heard 'round the world" were fired in Lexington, Massachusetts, and the war between the colonists and Great Britain was under way. At the outbreak of the Revolution, however, rural Americans were by no means reassured by the turn of events. As the Handlins write,

> In Maryland, small farmers feared independence would enslave the poor by putting all power into the hands of the rich, while some great landowners feared that removal of royal authority would open the way to anarchy and slave and tenant revolts. Other planters welcomed the separation that would free them from the obligation to repay debts to British merchants . . . and the unpredictable upheavals of war frightened all.
>
> In many places, opportunists held back, waiting to see which way the wind blew before choosing a flag. . . . Ordinary men and women weighed the threats of future retribution from London—whence came warnings that . . . [land] confiscations . . . and executions would be the reward of rebellion. . . . Concerned for their skins and possessions, they followed the dominant opinion of the district in order to be on the winning side.[23]

Fear and rumor swept through the countryside. Some said that the British hired fifty thousand fierce Russian soldiers known as Cossacks to take back the country. Others believed that the British were arming planta-

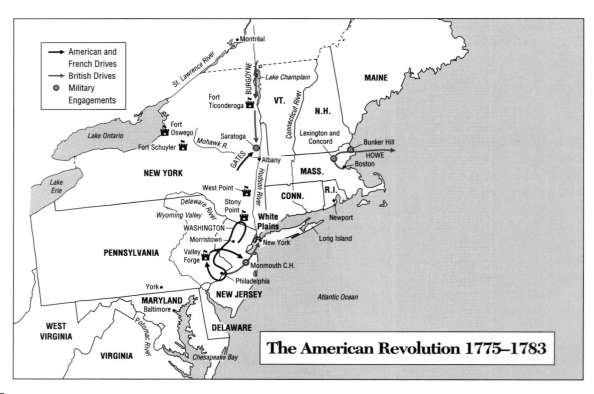

The American Revolution 1775–1783

Random Acts of Violence

Drunken British soldiers sometimes tortured or killed American farmers for entertainment. In *Personal Recollections of the American Revolution,* Lydia Minturn Post writes of one such incident that took place in New York in 1776.

"About thirty miles to the eastward, a countryman was met on the road by a company of English soldier ruffians, when they began to curse and swear, and threaten to compel him to say, "God save the king," which he resolutely and unwisely refused to do; though doubtless not counting on their putting their threat into execution. One of the villains, more in liquor and more violent than the rest, stepped up to the American, with a drawn sword, which he kept flourishing over the poor creature's head, and shouted, '*Say it, or by [God] you're a dead man!*' The villain paused an instant; the dumb silence of the man continued, and the dreadful threat was put into execution!

I suppose there are many around us who would have done the same thing. Few, in this our day and generation pray for their enemies, not even '*Good King George!*'"

tion slaves and Native Americans to fight battles against the colonists. In some rural regions, the Revolution turned into civil war as the patriots who supported independence formed militias to fight the loyalists who supported the British.

The War in the Countryside

Although the main battles of the Revolutionary War were fought in or around major American cities, rural areas saw action as well. In the countryside, patriots used a form of guerrilla warfare adopted from the Native Americans in which riflemen hid behind trees and rocks while raining gunfire down on British troops marching in formation along country lanes. To cause further troubles for these troops, according to Raphael, "The Americans chopped down trees and turned the roadways into swamps in order to slow the progress of the British; they also destroyed corn and drove off cattle to deny food to the enemy troops."[24]

Keeping the various armies stocked with provisions put a large strain on American agriculture workers. Even though few battles were fought in rural New England, the Continental Army desperately needed food from the area, and in 1780 New Hampshire, Massachusetts, and Connecticut were called on by Congress to provide four thousand head of cattle per month. Farmers were also asked to provide draft horses, oxen, and other beasts of burden to the army.

Some profiteering farmers charged inflated wartime prices or sold inferior products. For instance, they soaked meat in water to increase its weight, or passed off horse meat as beef. As one soldier wrote, "We many times have drawn Such Roten Stinkin meat that the Smell is Sufficient to make us loathe the same."[25]

Though many tried their best to supply the army at honest prices, agricultural life was complicated in the early years of the war, when the British won almost every battle and took control of vast areas of the East Coast. These soldiers, and their German allies, known as Hessians, wreaked havoc on the

General George Washington visits the wounded. The greatest hardship inflicted on the rural population was the loss of their fathers and sons to the cause, sometimes permanently.

countryside. Firewood was always in short supply, and the invading armies simply took what they wanted, as Lydia Minturn Post wrote in 1776 in *Personal Recollections of the American Revolution:*

> The Hessians have been ordered to cut down all the saplings they can find. They pile them along the road about twelve feet high, then by pressing teams and wagons, they cart it away to forts and barracks at a distance. It is a serious loss; in a few years our farms will be without wood for use. They [the Hessians] burn an immense quantity;—even the rail-fences, unless we take care to cut and cart wood for their constant use. Keeping the fire a-going all night, many a poor farmer rises in the morning to find his cattle strayed miles away, or his grain trampled down and ruined![26]

The occupation also disrupted the flow of goods to market, creating shortages of food, draft animals, wagons, and other farm necessities. Salt, used for preserving meat, was in such short supply that violence resulted when people were discovered hoarding the precious commodity.

The soldiers were often drunk and rowdy, accosting citizens as they performed their work in the fields. British redcoats sometimes demanded that patriot men swear allegiance to King George; those who did not answer fast enough could lose a limb, or even their head.

In addition, farmers were forced to deal with an occupying army that demanded food and lodging for soldiers and officers. Post described the acts of extremely intoxicated Hessians quartered in her home: "fighting, brawls, drumming and fifing, and dancing the night long; card and dice playing, and every abomination going on under our very roofs! The noise from the kitchen, which they always occupy, is terrifying."[27]

The greatest pain the war inflicted on rural households was, by far, the loss of fathers and sons to the army. Between 1775 and 1781, tens of thousands of farmers left their families to fight for freedom and liberty. Since labor was already in short supply, army recruitment aggravated an already difficult situation. And during the American Revolution, about four thousand soldiers died of

Drunken British soldiers sometimes demanded that patriots swear allegiance to the despised British monarch George III (pictured).

battle wounds and disease. Many of these were men who had once provided the food, tobacco, and other products that had made America prosperous and strong enough to stand up to the British army in the first place. The boyhood skills they had learned hunting grouse and deer near their backwoods homes had given them the collective power to put the British redcoats on the run.

The American Revolution was born in Boston, Massachusetts, and quickly spread through the port cities of the East Coast such as New York and Philadelphia. The people in these cities relied on the ocean for nourishment, employment, shipping, and travel. As Gary B. Nash writes in *The Urban Crucible: The Northern Seaports and the Origins of the American Revolution,*

> Water dominated the life of America's . . . seaport towns . . . providing them with links to the outer world, yielding up much of their sustenance, and . . . affecting the relationships among the different groups who made up these budding commercial capitals. Boston was built on a tadpole-shaped peninsula jutting into island-dotted Massachusetts Bay and was connected to the mainland only by a small mile-long causeway called the Neck. New York was literally an island, set in perhaps the finest natural harbor on the continent. . . . [People in these] colonial seaports gathered timber, fish, and agricultural produce from the rural

Philadelphia, as well as the other colonial port cities, was bustling, fast-paced and energetic on the eve of the Revolution.

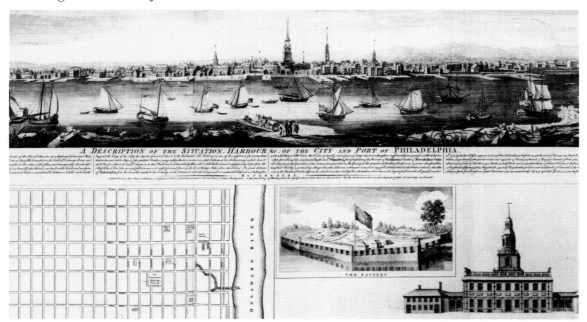

Before the hostilities put a stop to trade, merchants in New York City dealt with a wide array of products, as listed by an unnamed eighteenth-century source in *New York in the American Revolution* by Wilber C. Abbott.

"[From New York] to the West Indies went bread, pease, rye-meal, Indian corn, apples, onions, boards, staves, horses, sheep, butter, cheese, pickled oysters, beef and pork and eighty thousand barrels of flour a year, all inspected and branded to keep up the quality. [To New York] came chiefly rum, sugar and molasses, cash from Curaçao and mules from the Spanish Main. Wheat, flour, Indian corn and lumber shipped to Lisbon [Portugal] and Madeira [Spain], balance the Madeira wine imported; and these with the logwood trade with Honduras, the exportation of flax-seed to Ireland; the imports of linen; peltry of all kinds, purchased with rum, ammunition, blankets, and wampum; dry-goods from England, cotton from St. Thomas and Surinam, lime-juice and 'Nicaragua wood'; duck and chequered linen . . . cordage [fine rope] and tea from Hamburg and Holland, such were the commodities which made up the bulk of the New York business."

settlers who made up the vast majority of the continental population, sent it to West Indian and European markets, and distributed finished European goods throughout the regions they served.[28]

Busy Workers

On the eve of the Revolution the East Coast ports hummed with activity as ship captains steered towering, square-rigged ships in and out of the harbors night and day, their cargo holds filled with lumber, iron, furs, flaxseed, rice, indigo dyes, beer, butter, grain, pork, beef, cheese, and hundreds of other products. These goods were weighed and inspected by armies of British custom and tax agents who sat at large desks in the wooden warehouses that lined the wharves.

The docks rattled with the sounds of saws and hammers in shipyards where hundreds of men were employed to construct schooners, warships, and merchant vessels.

From nearly every country in the world, thousands of sailors, most of them between the ages of fifteen and twenty, traversed the docks. Those who had just arrived scurried to dockside taverns, gambling parlors, and houses of prostitution.

Back from the wharves, dozens of businesses catered to the shipping trade. In long wooden sheds called ropewalks, skilled rope makers spun hemp into the miles of mainstays, anchor cables, and other thick lines used on ships. In other cavernous warehouses sail makers laid out huge sheets of canvas to cut and stitch sails for ships.

Nearby, blacksmiths could be seen hunched over their anvils pounding red-hot iron into bolts, chains, anchors, hinges, iron bands, and hundreds of other metal items needed for shipping. Block makers constructed giant wooden and metal pulleys, and carpenters pounded together ladders, furnishings, lockers, and trunks for use on board. Craftsmen called chandlers supplied candles, whale oil, and lamps so sailors could see in the dark.

A master shipsmith, journeymen, and apprentices forge a ship's anchor.

Skilled metalworkers designed and built compasses, sextants, and chronometers so ships' captains could steer the proper course.

Even as the threat of war hung in the air, the pace of the docks barely slackened. As Revolutionary firebrand Sam Adams wrote about Boston,

> My Eyes are so diverted with Chimney Sweeps, Carriers of Wood, Merchants, Ladies, Priests, Carts, Horses, Oxen, Coaches, Market men and Women, Soldiers, Sailors, and my Ears with the Rattle Gabble of them all that . . . I can't raise my mind above this Crowd of Men, Women, Beasts and Carriages [to plan political actions].[29]

Home and Hearth

Although they were at the heart and soul of American enterprise—and the center for heated battles during the Revolution—the East Coast cities were small by modern standards. They had been growing continually, however, throughout the eighteenth century.

Between 1740 and 1760 the population of Philadelphia nearly doubled from thirteen thousand to almost twenty-four thousand. New York's population grew from eleven thousand to eighteen thousand. This increase was fueled by a steady flow of German, Scotch-Irish, English, Welsh, and Scottish immigrants. The new immigrants brought European culture and ideas of science and progress to American shores.

The influx of people created an unprecedented building boom in America's cities. Although Philadelphia had only fifteen hundred homes in 1743, the town doubled in size to three thousand dwellings by 1760. But even though new buildings were being added, old structures remained from the earliest years of the settlement. Impoverished new arrivals were often forced to live in crude log cabins located right next door to newly constructed mansions. In *Material Life in America 1600–1860*, Philip D. Morgan gives examples of the way people lived in Philadelphia in 1767:

> Laboring Philadelphians commonly crowded into small, narrow, wooden houses. [For example,] Philip Mager, a tailor with

a wife and four children, leased a two-story wooden tenement twelve feet wide and eighteen feet deep. Mariner Richard Crips and his family rented an eleven-by-fourteen foot, single-story dwelling in the northern suburbs. In his two-story wooden box, eighteen feet square, in Harmony Alley, tailor William Smith may have found himself in even more cramped quarters. Like many other poor men, he did not have a separate kitchen, so his wife prepared meals in the fireplace not only for their three children but also for two boarders. Many families saved expenses by taking in lodgers or by doubling up with other families. Laborer Martin Summers and his family, for example, lived with cordwainer [rope maker] Henry Birkey, his wife, and three children and divided the £18 annual rent. With his wife and four young children, Christian Fight . . . shared his abode and £12 lease with fellow shoemaker Christian Nail and his family. By contrast, wealthier citizens frequently occupied three-story brick houses . . . with such outbuildings as kitchens, wash houses, and stables. Many owned two-story brick kitchens of a size equal to or greater than most of the dwellings of the lower sort.[30]

Politics and Poverty

As soon as the French and Indian War ended in 1763 the British government began imposing taxes on imports and exports, sending a wave of bankruptcies through the port cities. In Boston the shipping trade fell by 80 percent, with similar dire consequences in New York. As one merchant complained, "Trade in this part of the world . . . is come to so wretched a pass that you would imagine the plague had been here."[31]

Meanwhile, about forty thousand British troops returned to England at the end of the hostilities. This had an immediate effect on the economic activities of city dwellers, as Nash writes: "English shillings no longer clanked into the tills of tavernkeepers and shop-owners. Instead former indentured servants and British deserters, many of them broken by army service, drifted into cities in search of employment."[32]

Philadelphia Home for Sale

A constant influx of immigrants spurred an ongoing building boom in America's port cities. In Philadelphia, the average private home was two or three stories high and made of brick or wood. In *Cities in Revolt: Urban Life in America, 1743–1776*, Carl Bridenbaugh includes a 1760s real estate ad for a Philadelphia home.

"Typical of the medium-sized establishments was Thomas Barton's, situated at the upper end of Front Street on a lot '20 Feet in Front, and 100 in Depth, 3 Stories high, with 3 Rooms on the first Floor and Fireplaces in each; the Front Room painted a fine Blue, the middle-Room a Slate Colour, and the rest a Chocolate Colour. This House . . . is likewise furnished with a large Stone Kitchen, and a spacious Cellar, good Water and a free open Air; it commands a fine Prospect, and is very fit for a private Gentleman, Shop-Keeper, or Tradesman.'"

Immigrants also continued to pour into the cities, resulting in housing and food shortages. There was also a scarcity of firewood, a necessity that urban families and businesses alike depended on to heat homes, cook meals, and fuel foundries and forges. As the forests surrounding cities were cut down the prices climbed even higher. On the eve of the Revolution firewood prices increased fivefold. As a result hundreds of people were forced to shiver in the cold in their own homes, unable to prepare hot meals.

During the unusually frigid winter of 1763–1764, the Committee to Alleviate the Miseries of the Poor was formed in Philadelphia to help people obtain firewood, clothing, and stockings. Volunteers went door to door to raise funds for the efforts, and newspapers ran editorials appealing for money. Meanwhile city poorhouses, known as almshouses, were filled with indigent citizens who lacked basic necessities such as food and clothing. One such facility in Philadelphia was so crowded that one worker wrote that the poor were jammed "into rooms but ten or eleven Feet square . . . [and into those rooms we] have been obliged to crowd five or six Beds."[33]

Stamp Act Riots

If American citizens were more prosperous in 1765, when the Stamp Act went into effect, there might not have been a revolution. But raising taxes on an already suffering populace pushed many formerly law-abiding citizens toward rebellion. As a judge in Philadelphia wrote, "The labouring People, and others in low circumstances . . . who are willing to work, cannot obtain sufficient Employment to support themselves and their Families."[34] And with high unemployment, thousands of men had no other place to go but the streets to voice their concerns.

The troubles began immediately after the hated Stamp Act was passed on August 14, 1765. Three straw-stuffed dummies, known as effigies, were found hanging from an elm tree in Boston's working-class neighborhood called South End. One effigy represented stamp distributor Andrew Oliver; the others were of two British politicians who helped pass the act. When the sheriff tried to cut down the effigies, he was surrounded by an angry mob who took to the streets. By midday thousands of people had gathered to protest British policies.

In *Crowd Action in Revolutionary Massachusetts 1765–1780,* Dirk Hoerder describes how the city people at the protest spread the message to the country folk:

> While the boys were waving flags, adults could participate in simulating the harassment that would result from the [Stamp] act. No farmer or teamster was allowed to enter or leave Boston without stopping to get his goods stamped. In an "enthusiastic spirit" the people good-humoredly mock-stamped all goods on the passing carts and wagons. It was relatively unimportant that the act referred to paper only and not to other goods. What was important was to reach large segments of the population, and teamsters and farmers, not accustomed to these delays, would definitely spread the story.[35]

As night fell, a twenty-eight-year-old shoemaker named Ebenezer MacIntosh cut down the effigies and led a crowd to the wharves, where Oliver's stamp collection office was torn down brick by brick. Jovial protesters "stamped" the demolished timbers in jest. The crowd then moved to a hill high above Oliver's home where they gathered around a huge bonfire, made speeches, and sang songs. The mood of the crowd turned ugly when Oliver's brother-in-law, royal governor Thomas Hutchinson, urged them to go home. Instead the crowd swarmed down the hill into Oliver's stables and destroyed his carriage. When they were done they smashed down the doors to his lavish home, broke the windows, stole dozens of bottles of expensive wine from the cellar, and destroyed the manicured gardens. The next day Oliver resigned as stamp distributor.

Twelve days later the homes of several government stamp officials were ransacked. The crowd, once again led by MacIntosh, then turned on Hutchinson's mansion. According to Nash,

Catching [Hutchinson] and his family at the dinner table, the crowd smashed in the doors with axes, sent the family packing, and then systematically reduced the furniture to splinters, stripped the walls bare, chopped through inner partitions until the house was a hollow shell, destroyed the formal gardens in the rear of

Enforcement of the Stamp Act triggered riots in working-class neighborhoods like Boston's South End.

The Boston Tea Party

The Boston Tea Party was pivotal in the events leading up to the Revolutionary War.

In December 1773, the Boston Tea Party set into motion a series of events that would lead to the Revolutionary War. The following is an eyewitness account of the Tea Party, written by an anonymous participant and published on the History Place website.

"[I] dressed myself in the costume of an Indian, equipped with a small hatchet, which I and my associates denominated the tomahawk . . . and a club. [After] having painted my face and hands with coal dust in the shop of a blacksmith, I repaired to Griffin's wharf, where the ships lay that contained the tea. When I first appeared in the street after being thus disguised, I fell in with many who were dressed, equipped and painted as I was, and who fell in with me and marched in order to the place of our destination. . . .

We were immediately ordered by the respective commanders to board all the ships at the same time, which we promptly obeyed. . . .

We then were ordered by our commander to open the hatches and take out all the chests of tea and throw them overboard, and we immediately proceeded to execute his orders, first cutting and splitting the chests with our tomahawks, so as thoroughly to expose them to the effects of the water.

In about three hours from the time we went on board, we had thus broken and thrown overboard every tea chest to be found in the ship, while those in the other ships were disposing of the tea in the same way, at the same time. We were surrounded by British armed ships, but no attempt was made to resist us."

the mansion, drank the wine cellar dry, stole £900 sterling in coin, and carried off objects of value. Led by MacIntosh, the crowd worked with almost military precision to raze the building.[36]

The scene resembled a war zone, and according to Boston citizen William Gordon, "Gentlemen of the army, who have seen towns sacked by the enemy, declared they never before saw an instance of such fury."[37]

And so the revolution of the working class against the rich and powerful began. The rioting against the Stamp Act resumed on October 31 in New York City, when a mob surrounded Governor Cadwallader Colden's house, hanged him in effigy, and put his gilded carriage to the torch. A written message was delivered to the governor, informing him: "You'll die a Martyr to your own Villainy, and be Hang'd . . . upon a Signpost, as a Memento to all wicked Governors that every Man that assists you, Shall be, surely, put to Death."[38]

In March 1766 the Stamp Act was repealed, and the mobs rejoiced. For the first time in American history a protest movement had reversed a government policy. The troubles were far from over, however. In 1767, the Townshend Act went into effect; the next year, British troops occupied Boston. As with the Stamp Act, these actions would inflame large crowds of unemployed dockworkers, shopkeepers near bankruptcy, and hundreds of people forced to live on charity in city almshouses.

Ale and Revolutionary Politics

The Sons of Liberty coordinated the protests against British policy, and their activities were based in taverns where ale flowed as freely as talk of revolution. Since most people lived in

The Revolution was born in tavern rooms like this one in Lexington, Massachusetts.

small homes, taverns, with their big open rooms, were the only place large groups such as the Sons could meet. It was in barrooms such as the Indian King Tavern and the Green Dragon Tavern that the Sons of Liberty made speeches, planned protests and boycotts, and drew up statements that were later printed on political handbills known as broadsides. In 1770 a loyalist in a New York tavern wrote about a Sons of Liberty meeting before the group took to the streets in protest:

> After carousing and drinking very plentifully and heating themselves with Liquor, in the glorious cause of Liberty, as they call it, they sallied out into the evening to put their [protest] in execution, carrying with them musick, colours and staff, which were labels fixed with the inscription of Liberty and Non-Importation.[39]

Although loyalists were disdainful of the Sons of Liberty, tavern owners actively courted the revolutionaries. Tavern keepers were usually from the same social class as the average worker, and they were also hurt by the Stamp Act because the taxes inflated the costs of liquor licenses, playing cards, dice, and other tools of the tavern trade. In addition, during the hard economic times, keeping bars full of impassioned patriots was good for business. Some places, like the Ballardville Tavern in Andover, Massachusetts, advertised for business by boldly writing on their wooden sign "For the Entertainment of the Sons of Liberty."[40]

One of the most famous drinking establishments of the Revolution was the three-story City Tavern, built in 1773, in Philadelphia. This bar was the central meeting place for the men who led the Revolution, including George Washington, John Adams, and Thomas Jefferson. In 1774 the First Continental Congress met often at the City Tavern to plan protests against British policies and put together a boycott against British imported goods.

In Trenton, New Jersey, another tavern doubled as a governmental meeting place, as Hoag Levins writes:

> Throughout 1777, the Indian King Tavern, with its huge second-floor meeting hall, served as a major political and administrative center for the Continental war effort. The Council and General Assembly of New Jersey —the state's main government body—was forced to evacuate its offices in the battle-ravaged Trenton and temporarily relocate to the Indian King. It was here that the Declaration of Independence was formally read into the minutes of the New Jersey Assembly. And it was here—with [tavern keeper] Hugh Creighton and staff serving up great tankards of ale for toasting afterward—that the Assembly enacted the law that officially changed New Jersey from a colony into a state and adopted that State's Great Seal.[41]

The Battle in Boston

In April 1775 the plots and protests by the Sons of Liberty erupted into war as the first battles of the Revolution took place in the villages of Lexington and Concord, Massachusetts. After the brief skirmish military strategists focused on Boston, where twenty-six hundred battle-hardened British soldiers tried to capture Breed's Hill from the patriots on June 17, 1775.

As nearly every citizen in town watched from hills and rooftops, the British redcoats, or "lobster backs," rowed ashore in barges with their flags and bright banners waving. Even before the shooting started the British

The British burned the homes and churches of Charlestown in full view of the citizens of Boston. The experience haunted Bostonians long after the event.

commanders, claiming that their troops were being harassed by snipers from nearby buildings, ordered the four hundred houses of Charlestown on the southern part of a peninsula known as "the Neck" to be set aflame. The town was engulfed in a conflagration within minutes. The sight was spectacular and horrible, as Continental soldier Jonathan Brigham later remembered:

> The awful solemnities of the day are still deeply impressed upon [my] mind . . . and the scenes of carnage and death and the inconceivable grandeur of the immense volume of flames illuminating the [Bunker Hill] battlefield from the burning of Charlestown appear as vivid as the events of yesterday.[42]

During the battle, 145 Americans and 226 British were killed, and hundreds more wounded. The destruction of Charlestown haunted Boston citizens long after the soldiers had moved on, as Donald Barr Chidsey writes in *The Siege of Boston:*

> Not only were some 400 good solid houses and a large number of churches burned to the ground, but many heirlooms, books, and irreplaceable family records that [patriots] in Boston had stored in the cellars of friends in Charlestown for fear that in the city they would be seized—they too were lost. . . . The British . . . to many Americans had . . . showed themselves too eager to burn Charlestown, perhaps if only to throw the fear of God into the patriots.[43]

The British Occupy Boston

After the Battle of Bunker Hill the people of Boston were forced to live under wartime conditions. Donald Barr Chidsey describes how the city suffered in *The Siege of Boston.*

"The British did a great deal of drilling, right out on the Boston Common and especially on the Charlestown Common, which could readily be seen from the American lines, and they also held many boat drills with small craft from the war vessels. These may have been meant only to keep the men busy . . . or they could have been intended to frighten the rebels. If the latter was the case, they could be said to succeed. . . .

The British would start a bombardment of Plowed Hill or Roxbury or wherever, every time, it would seem, that they happened to think of it, perhaps for the purpose of proving how much gunpowder and how many [cannon] balls they had. . . .

It had been an exceptionally warm summer, but even salted food must be cooked, and long before the leaves began to turn the supply of firewood in Boston was running low. Rail fences disappeared overnight, and trees were surreptitiously chopped down. Prices went up, and especially the price of cordwood, when you could get any at all. The British had converted the Old South Church into a riding academy but even they would hardly dare to tear down the houses of Boston one by one. Yet—how else were they to keep warm when winter came?

The smallpox epidemic had not abated, but rather increased, and now that fresh food was in such short supply scurvy, understandably, was prevalent. It was a debilitating disease that made the eyes sunken, the gums spongy and bloody, the muscles all one ache. Men did not often die of scurvy, but they suffered horribly—and they stank. It was a most unpleasant malady to nurse."

The War in New York City

Although the British won the first battle in Boston, by March the ragtag, poorly trained Continental Army had succeeded in driving them from that town. The focus of the war then shifted to Manhattan Island as twenty thousand American troops marched into New York, a beautiful city later described by a Hessian soldier known only as Captain Hinrichs:

New York's island is the prettiest place I have ever seen. There is not a superfluous tree, not a useless twig, not an unserviceable straw on it. Fruitful sloping hills alternate with tillage land, meadows, and gardens full of fruit trees; and single houses, built on the heights [of] both sides of the river, give the eye a charming view. All are painted white, [three stories tall], with *verandahs,* and upstairs a balcony and lightning-rods: moreover, all are built and furnished in the best of taste.[44]

With the arrival of the Continental Army, however, pastoral Manhattan was turned into an armed camp. Trees were torn down, and stone walls were carted off to build fortifications. Public buildings, such as King's College, were converted to military barracks and hospitals. Parks were turned into parade grounds and warehouses made into barracks. Many New York City residents were British loyalists and were extremely frightened by the patriot invasion. Loyalist Prussian pastor Ewald Gustav Schaukirk described the scene in April 1775:

> The past week has been one of commotion and confusion. Trade and public business was at a [standstill]; soldiers were enlisted; the inhabitants seized the keys of the Custom House; and arms and powder were taken from the [warehouse]. Fear and panic seized many of the people, who prepared to move into the country.[45]

Soldiers in the disorganized Continental Army continued to disrupt life throughout the summer, marching, firing their guns, and drinking, prompting Schaukirk to write,

> The Minute men paraded today, with their baggage and provisions. It was thought they were going on an expedition, but they marched but five miles out of the city and returned in the evening. Many of them got drunk, fought together where they had halted, and on their return, the Doctors and Surgeons were kept busy. May the Lord have mercy on this poor City![46]

By August the army occupation had caused between one-half and two-thirds of New Yorkers to leave town. Schaukirk wrote, "some of the Streets look plague-stricken, so many houses are closed."[47]

Around that time thirty thousand British soldiers and German Hessians landed in the New York City area. No larger fighting force had ever been assembled anywhere on earth during the eighteenth century, and by November, the Continental Army was on the run, having suffered major defeats at a loss of thousands of lives. For the remainder of the war New York City was the center for

British military operations in the American colonies, and the city would remain under British control until the war officially ended in 1783.

With the British victory, the patriots fled the city, while loyalists took over their homes and businesses. Six days after the British took over New York, a fire started in the oldest section of town, destroying nearly 25 percent of the homes on Manhattan Island.

For the average citizen, life, which was already difficult, became even worse. Foods such as meat, milk, grain, and produce were in short supply. The prices of basic necessities such as clothing and firewood skyrocketed. Meanwhile the British officers lived as if they were royalty, taking over public spaces and private homes for their personal use, as Schaukirk writes:

> [The] military gentlemen amuse themselves with trifles and diversions. Recently the walk by the ruins of Trinity Church and its grave-yard has been [fenced] in and painted green; benches placed there and many lamps fixed in the trees, for gentlemen and ladies to walk and sit there in the evening. A band plays while the commander is present, and a sentry is placed there, that none of the common people may intrude. A paltry affair! A house opposite is adapted to accommodate the ladies or officer's women, while many honest people, both . . . the inhabitants and Refugees cannot get a house or lodging to live in or get their living.[48]

The War in Philadelphia

While British officers amused themselves in New York City, the war moved southwest to Pennsylvania. On September 26, 1777, the

British were able to conquer Philadelphia. While British loyalists thronged in the streets to greet the victorious general Lord Howe, nearly ten thousand American patriots fled America's largest city.

Meanwhile Washington's troops set up blockades on the roads leading into Philadelphia to prevent the British from entering the countryside to buy provisions. As had happened elsewhere, city food prices soared and shortages ensued. Although the blockade most affected the poor, it was also felt by middle-class Philadelphians whose gardens and cattle were taken by foragers. According to John W. Jackson in *With the British Army in Philadelphia 1777–1778*,

> The Hessians swarmed over the area, digging up potatoes, turnips, and other vegetables. Ten or more soldiers would take over a garden, working alongside the owner as he harvested his crops; if he protested, they would threaten him, declaring there was enough for all. The next day wives of these soldiers were seen sitting in the market house selling the products of their thievery. At night Hessian soldiers slinked out to private property and stole cattle, slaughtered them, and the next day offered the meat for sale. The Hessian looting, however, was petty thievery compared to the cupidity of certain British soldiers and civilians. Fleeing American families had deserted their homes, with a number left fully furnished. Furniture and other articles left behind were confiscated and sold at public [auction]. One informant stated an occasional vacant house was sold by the British to incoming refugees.[49]

As the winter wore on even pilfered foods disappeared from markets, and most Philadel-phians had little to eat but flour and rancid beef. The lack of vegetables, eggs, butter, cheese, and milk severely affected the health of the people, and hundreds died of various diseases. Even the wealthiest citizens found it difficult to meet their most basic needs. In January 1778 Captain Hinrichs wrote about how the lack of food was affecting people both physically and psychologically:

> Among a hundred people . . . in Philadelphia . . . not one has a healthy color. . . . Nothing is commoner here than a fever once a year, and then skin-irruptions, itch, etc. Nowhere have I found such a lot of madmen as here. Just yesterday I was eating with a gentleman, when a third person came into the room and whispered in my ear: Take care, this gentleman is a madman. Often the people are cured again, but almost all have a quiet madness, an aberration of the mind. . . . One reason is perhaps that no food here has the same strength as with us at home. The milk is not half so rich, the bread gives little strength.[50]

The citizens were also suffering from the bitter winter cold because the British confiscated at least six hundred blankets from local residents while tearing up fences and chopping down groves of trees for firewood. Although most complained bitterly about sacrificing their timbers for firewood, some loyalists provided it as a show of patriotic duty, according to Hinrichs: "One man from the city here named *Hamilton* alone has lost fifteen hundred acres of wood . . . and yet he had patriotism enough to remark at a gathering recently that it was for the good of the country."[51]

While some sacrificed their woodlands for the loyalists, others worked as spies to

After the British evacuated Philadelphia, General Washington paraded prisoners through the streets to the cheers of the local populace.

help the patriots, eavesdropping on British soldiers and sending messages to General Washington. The escapades of the Darragh family were detailed on a Central Intelligence Agency website that explores the spy activities of the Revolutionary War:

Officers of the British force occupying Philadelphia chose to use a large upstairs room in the Darragh house for conferences. When they did, Mrs. Darragh would slip into an adjoining closet and take notes on the enemy's military plans. Her husband, William, would transcribe the intelligence in a form of shorthand on tiny slips of paper that Lydia would then position on a button mold before covering it with fabric. The message-bearing buttons were then sewn onto the coat of her fourteen-year-old son, John, who would then be sent to visit his elder brother, Lieutenant Charles Darragh, of the American forces outside the city. Charles would snip off the buttons and transcribe the shorthand notes into readable form for presentation to his officers. Lydia Darragh is said to have concealed other intelligence in a sewing-needle packet which she carried in her purse when she passed through British lines.[52]

Despite the activities of the Darraghs and others, the twenty thousand British troops were forced to evacuate Philadelphia after a nineteen-month occupation only because of tactical blunders in battles fought elsewhere. In June 1778 as they left, they destroyed wharves and bridges and threw barrels of salted pork and beef into the Delaware River. At least four thousand blankets from army hospitals were burned in a huge bonfire. So that they would not aid the Continental Army, every ship under construction in the harbor was burned to the waterline, along with the shipyards themselves. As the flames burned for days, they also devoured homes of the poor who lived nearby.

In their hasty retreat the British left many supplies behind, including seven thousand gallons of rum and one thousand gallons of brandy. Philadelphians were also relieved to find packages of medicine, barrels of molasses, and twelve thousand bushels of salt. Excess wood and hay was sold by officers or, in some cases, given to the poor.

When Washington and his army came back to town, chaos once again reigned as homes and businesses were abandoned and loyalists fled the city. As Jackson writes,

> The anger of the returning Americans increased as they saw the debris and filth that littered the city's streets. With the British army gone, the logical targets for censure or revenge were hapless Loyalists. Moderates and radicals among the Americans agreed that all Loyalists who had consorted with or joined the British army or navy were guilty of treason, and that their estates should be confiscated.[53]

The Ravages of War

Although Americans had gained their freedom from the British rulers, average citizens suffered to a much greater extent than their wealthier neighbors, as Raphael writes:

> As hard as they worked, common folk had less to consume. Time and again, they made do without—at first voluntarily [in protest], later not. The temporary hardships of nonimportation were followed by severe wartime scarcities which spanned the better part of a decade. The colonies, with a limited manufacturing capacity, made ships, arms, and ammunition instead of useful tools and consumer goods. Salt, required to preserve food, was requisitioned by the American, British, German, and French armies; people rioted over what little was left for civilian use. . . .

> Common people endured the ravages of war. They were pillaged by the various armies in their midst. Women were raped. Homes were commandeered for the use of officers. Houses were burned, fences destroyed. Diseases ran rampant: more people died of illnesses spread by the war than did from enemy fire.[54]

In the end, the people of Boston, New York City, Philadelphia, and elsewhere had paid the price of war. They would be remembered by future generations for sacrificing their comfort, property, and even their lives for the cause of liberty.

Lives of Revolutionary Soldiers

Although the Revolutionary War affected the lives of more than 2 million Americans, it was fought one battle at a time in geographically distant locations by armies that rarely numbered more than ten thousand per side.

The Revolution is often remembered by the words and deeds of great statesmen like Franklin, Jefferson, and Adams, but it was the average man with his musket and sword who did the dirty work of taking on the British in battle after battle. And this difficult and dangerous work was largely performed by soldiers between the ages of fifteen and twenty. Boys as young as eleven and men over the age of fifty also were occasionally recruited for military service. In *The Book of the Continental Soldier*, Harold L. Peterson describes the American soldiers assembled in Boston in 1775:

> [It] was truly a motley [group], more a mob than an army. It had sprung into existence almost spontaneously as the various local minutemen, alarm companies, and volunteers had pursued the British troops and their retreat from Concord and Lexington. . . . For the first few weeks chaos was almost complete with no overall command, no definite enlistments, and only such discipline as the natural decency of the men provided. . . .

> Discipline was lax, and . . . this was especially noticeable among [the] riflemen

The typical infantryman in the Continental Army was most often a young man between the ages of fifteen and twenty.

who disobeyed orders and openly mutinied on one occasion. Worst of all there was no overall plan for an army, no table of organization. All these situations had to be corrected as speedily as possible in the face of an enemy and while appealing to the patriotism of the men.[55]

This ragtag group of farm boys, craftsmen, recent immigrants, and indentured servants faced off against one of the most battle-hardened armies anywhere in the world. When the war began in 1775, many of the red-coated British soldiers had recently seen hand-to-hand combat in France, Spain, Holland, and India against professional soldiers of a much higher caliber than the rebels could ever hope to muster. And the British brought along professional help; of the more than fifty-five thousand soldiers shipped to the colonies between 1770 and 1781, more than thirty thousand were Hessian mercenaries. With thousands of Native Americans, slaves, and American loyalists added to their ranks, the British constantly outnumbered the American fighting men, sometimes two to one.

Responding to the "Powder Alarms"

Before the first shots erupted in 1775, patriots in villages, towns, and cities throughout Massachusetts began preparing for war, training men and stockpiling gunpowder, supplies, and weapons. In *An Original and Authentic Journal of Occurrences During the Late American War,* Roger Lamb, a British soldier, witnessed the ardor and efficiency with which the patriots pursued their cause:

The sound of drums and fifes every where [*sic*] saluted the ear. Parents and children, husbands and lovers, the young and the old, were possessed of the same martial spirit. Nothing was to be seen or heard of, but the purchasing of arms and ammunition, casting of [cannon] balls, and the making of all those preparations, which testify the most immediate danger and determined resistance; and to render themselves independent of foreigners for the supply of military stores, they erected mills and manufactures for gunpowder.[56]

Such activity did not go unnoticed by British authorities, who coordinated missions into the countryside to search for and destroy the weapons caches. To prepare for these incursions, the patriots trained for "powder alarms" in which the militia could be called on to fight at a moment's notice.

On September 1, 1775, in a surprise operation, the British seized weapons caches in Cambridge and Charlestown. Rumors swept through the countryside that the British navy was raining cannonballs down on Boston, and according to an eyewitness account by Joseph Plumb Martin in *Adventures of a Revolutionary Soldier,* another rumor reported that "the British . . . regulars . . . were advancing from Boston, spreading death and desolation in their route in every direction."[57]

Before this rumor could be put to rest, thousands of men from Massachusetts and the neighboring colonies picked up arms and began marching toward the patriot capital in a spontaneous show of patriotism. Reverend Stephen Williams described the uproar in the village of Longmeadow when the rumor swept through that town during the middle of his church service:

After we had got to the meeting house in the afternoon . . . [a parishioner] came in & informd that they had news from

Boston—that the Ships in the Harbour of Boston, & the Army on the Land Side were allso fireing upon the Town so that it was like the Town was Demolishd. . . . People were put into a tumult & I closd the prayer—& Great numbers went out. . . .

The blacksmith shop was opend—guns carrid to him to be mendd—horses to be Shod—& many Employd makeing Bullets—& a man Sent to . . . get [gun]powdr—in the Evening people met again, & repaird to the meeting house—& a number Gave in their names or listd & chose Some leader and were Getting ready to move—but while they were togather at the meeting house—Mr. J. Sykes, came again to them & informd that the messenger was returnd & brot tideings—that all was well, and quiet at Boston—that there had been a tumult, or Squabble at Boston—& one man Killd—but now quiet & Still—oh how have we [sinned] away, & misimprovd [the] Sabboth.[58]

Although a battle never ensued, these "powder alarms" became all too common in the months before the war. In February 1775, when several hundred redcoats tried to march into Salem to seize an arms cache, they were turned back by hundreds of screaming, musket-waving citizens of the town. After a shouting match, the British backed down.

The Shots Heard 'Round the World

On April 19, 1775, the British attempted to seize a large supply of military hardware and powder hidden in Concord, about twenty miles west of Boston. This mission was attempted at eleven o'clock at night, as Lamb writes: "Wishing to accomplish this without bloodshed, [we] took every precaution to effect it by surprise, without alarming the country."[59]

The British were discovered, however, by the minutemen who began firing guns and

The British redcoats marched into Lexington in platoons led by officers on horseback. They were easy targets for colonists firing from farmhouse windows and from behind trees.

The Battle of Lexington

On the Military History Online website, the Battle of Lexington is recounted by J.D. Miller.

"As a response to hearing the hearsay of possible revolts, Major General Thomas Gage, the commander of all British forces in North America . . . orders a column of seven hundred men to demolish the weaponry depot at Concord. The column is under the command of . . . Major John Pitcairn. . . .

Back in Boston, before seeing the total advance, Paul Revere makes his famous ride, which stops at Lexington to warn the patriots of the oncoming British regulars. Captain John Parker, who is in command of the minutemen and militia at Lexington, watches as a scout, Thaddeus Bowman, gallops with his horse over the rise and reports the situation. Bowman reports that . . . there are almost a thousand of them, and that the redcoats are over an hour away, and quickly approaching. . . . Knowing that the regulars will soon be upon them, Parker orders his men to disperse and hide in the underbrush.

With the arrival of the full British column . . . the minutemen still in the underbrush, are found out by the regulars, and instead of a formal parley, the regulars, about thirty of them, come running out to the underbrush and yell 'damn them, we will have them!'

[A] single . . . shot rang out from behind a stone wall . . . unknown from which musket the shot came from.

Responding, the British fire without orders. Next, they get into line formation and begin pouring volley upon volley into the minutemen. Finally, the regulars turn the firing into a full-fledged charge. Lt. Colonel Smith himself must then ride out into the field and stop the charge. The British killed eight minutemen, and wounded nine others. The war has begun."

Hand-to-hand fighting is depicted here in the Battle of Lexington.

ringing bells. Fleeing the town, the redcoats marched all night until they reached Lexington at five o'clock in the morning. Ringing bells in Lexington warned bootmaker and minuteman Sylvanus Wood that the British were coming. Wood awoke, grabbed his gun, and ran to the town square. Lining up with hundreds of other men in single file in order to display a show of force, Wood and the other patriots did not expect violence. But, as Wood writes,

> The British troops approached us rapidly in platoons, with a general officer on horseback at their head. The officer came up to within about two rods of the center of the company where I stood, the first platoon being about three rods distant. There they halted. The officer then swung his sword, and said, "Lay down your arms, you damned rebels, or you are all dead men. Fire!" Some guns were fired by the British at us from the first platoon, but no person was killed or hurt, being probably charged only with powder.

> Just at this time, [minuteman] Captain Parker ordered every man to take care of himself. The company immediately dispersed; and while the company was dispersing and leaping over the wall, the second platoon of the British fired, and killed some of our men. There was not a gun fired by any of Captain Parker's company, within my knowledge. I was so situated that I must have known it, had anything of the kind taken place.[60]

Although a few patriots were killed, as the British marched back to Boston, colonists — both male and female—fired on the redcoats from farmhouse windows and from behind trees. The Revolutionary War had begun.

Summer Patriots

After the Battle of Bunker Hill in June 1775, crowds of men from across New England poured into Boston, driven by visions of patriotic glory. The Continental Congress authorized a plan for an army with twenty-six regiments, totaling more than twenty thousand men. Unfortunately, as the realities of military service set in, the recruiting effort was beset with problems. Few men could afford to leave their wives, families, and farms for a period of sixteen months. Those who did worried constantly about their affairs back home, as Joseph Hodgkins wrote to his wife, Sarah: "I whant to know wether you have got a [pasture] for the Cows for I cannot tell when I shall com home."[61]

By March fewer than ten thousand men had been recruited, about half as many as were necessary for victory. Meanwhile the British and American armies found themselves in a standoff in the hills around Boston, occasionally engaging in small scattered scuffles. Few were killed or injured in these skirmishes, but hundreds of soldiers were subsequently felled by typhoid fever and dysentery that swept through the crowded, filthy military camps. As one soldier wrote, "[The] numbers of . . . men are daily diminishing; they . . . are sickly, filthy, divided and unruly; putrid disorders, the small pox in particular, have carried off great numbers."[62] The sick were taken to makeshift military hospitals. Those who did not die often limped home, where they spread the epidemic among their friends and families.

As winter approached, patriotism and enthusiasm for military glory quickly evaporated among the American soldiers, few of whom considered themselves professional fighting men. In addition, lack of clothing posed a real problem for the volunteers. Officers wore bits and pieces of old uniforms they had obtained, some dating back to the French and Indian War of the 1750s. The enlisted men often wore their workclothes. Simeon Alexander, who served three terms with Massachusetts militia, described the dress of those serving under Captain Daniel Morgan:

> The uniform of Morgan's regiment was a short frock made of pepper-and-salt colored cotton cloth like a common working frock worn by our country people, except that it was opened [in front], to be tied with strings, pantaloons of the same fabric and color, and some kind of cap. . . . This was their summer dress.[63]

By September Washington reported to Congress that nearly half of his men had expressed the will to leave the army. As Hodgkins wrote, "at Presant . . . our People are all most Bewitcht about getting home."[64]

Recruiting Soldiers

As the first troops left in droves, a high priority was placed on recruitment. And as the harsh reality of a soldier's life became obvious, there were fewer and fewer who were willing to sacrifice their lives for the cause.

Since there was no draft the Continental Army was forced to rely on volunteers. To overcome the shortage of man power, Congress authorized recruiters to promise decent food and clothing to volunteers, and to offer signing bonuses and free land to those who enlisted. To aid in recruitment, posters were placed in thousands of taverns. One issued in George Washington's name read,

> To all brave, healthy, able bodied, and well disposed young men, in this neighbourhood, who have any inclination to join the troops, now raising under General Wash-

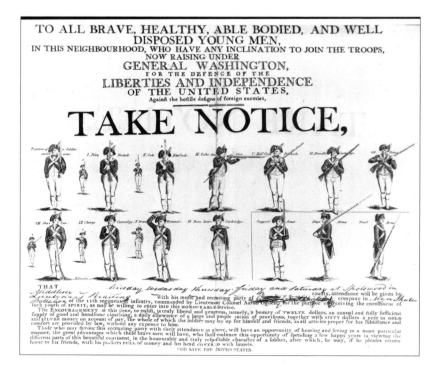

A recruitment notice urges patriotic young men to join in the defense of their country.

Scruffy new recruits for the revolutionary forces are drilled in front of amused locals.

ington for the defence of the liberties and independence of the United States, against a hostile dohgma of foreign enemies, take notice. . . . The ENCOURAGEMENT at this time, to enlist, is truly liberal and generous, namely a bounty of TWELVE dollars, an annual and fully sufficient supply of good and handsome clothing, a daily allowance of a large and ample ration of provisions, together with SIXTY dollars a year in gold and silver money . . . [and] the opportunity of spending a few happy years in viewing the different parts of this beautiful continent [and returning home] with his pocket FULL of money and his head COVERED with laurels.[65]

Despite the flowery language on the recruiting broadsheets, recruitment was not easy. After the poster campaign army captains traveled from town to town, cornering young men in local taverns, buying them drinks, and appealing to their patriotism. The recruiters hoped to get a few young men so intoxicated that they would sign the proffered military papers.

Younger boys, those under the age of sixteen, were easiest to recruit—and the easiest to

Difficulties Recruiting Soldiers

To fill the ranks in the Continental Army, military recruiters combed the taverns of the countryside in search of volunteers. One such recruiter, Captain Alexander Graydon, wrote about this difficult task in 1776 in *Memoirs of a Life, Chiefly Passed in Pennsylvania.*

"A number of fellows at the tavern . . . indicated a desire to enlist, but although they drank freely of our liquor, they still held off. I soon perceived that the object was to amuse themselves at our expense. . . . One fellow in particular . . . began to grow insolent, and manifested an intention to begin a quarrel, in the issue of which, he no doubt calculated on giving us a drubbing. . . . I resolved, that if a scuffle should be unavoidable, it should, at least, be as serious as the hangers [swords] which my lieu-tenant and myself carried by our sides, could make it. . . . At length the arrogance of the principal ruffian, rose to such a height, that he squared himself for battle and advanced towards me in an attitude of defiance. . . . The occasion was soon presented; when taking excellent aim, I struck him with the utmost force between the eyes and sent him staggering to the other end of the room. Then instantly drawing our hangers . . . we were fortunate enough to put a stop to any further hostilities. . . . This incident would be little worthy of relating, did it not serve in some degree to correct the error of those who seem to conceive the year 1776 to have been a season of almost universal patriotic enthusiasm. It was far from prevalent in my opinion, among the lower ranks of the people, at least in Pennsylvania."

train. Recruiters often downplayed the threat to these boys, as sixteen-year-old Samuel Shelley reported: "Colonel Dickinson . . . came up to me and said 'Sam, join us for nine months and then maybe the war will be over.'"[66]

Recruiters who did not work the taverns hired bands to play on street corners under waving flags. As the crowd gathered to see what the commotion was about, the recruiters handed out whiskey and tried to persuade the drunken men to join the army. Those who did not volunteer might be dragged off against their will, waking up with a hangover in a military camp wondering how they got there.

Obviously this process did not attract the pinnacle of colonial manhood. In *Memoirs of a Life, Chiefly Passed in Pennsylvania,* Captain Alexander Graydon wrote about one scoundrel he signed, "a fellow . . . [who] would do to stop a bullet as well as a better

man, and as he was a truly worthless dog . . . the neighborhood would be much indebted to us for taking him away."[67]

Hungry Troops

Raising an army was only part of the problem faced by patriot leaders. Soldiers did not have enough weapons, gunpowder, or bullets to go forth and fight. In addition, the troops desperately needed blankets, uniforms, tools, tents, cooking supplies, and other necessities.

To remedy the initial problem of feeding the troops, Washington used some of the meager funds provided by Congress to obtain fifteen thousand barrels of flour. This supply was augmented by thousands of hogs that were purchased from local farmers and driven to the outskirts of Boston, where soldiers went to work slaughtering the animals and salting the meat.

Despite these efforts, the soldiers were ill equipped and underclothed for most of the war. They froze in the cold, were drenched in the rain, and often had only rock-hard biscuits to eat. Many became violently sick from rancid meat, bad water, and infectious diseases. Richard Vining, an indentured servant who joined the army, describes his unappetizing food situation and the hardships he faced while marching to invade Quebec in the frigid autumn of 1775:

The general . . . procured a cow and sent [it] back to relieve the army. Previous to this, our company was obliged to kill a dog and eat it for our breakfast, and in the course of that day I killed an owl, and two of my messmates and myself [ate it]. However, we came up with the cow and cooked a portion of it and drinked the broth of the beef and owl cooked together, and the next day eat the meat. The second day after we got the beef, it rained heavily and turned to a snowstorm, and the snow fell [knee] deep. The day following . . . we came soon to a house where we drew a pound of beef and three potatoes each. . . . Next day started, and I was taken sick of a kind of camp distemper. Could not walk far in a day. Went on five miles and came to another house where we got one pound of beef, three potatoes, and a pint of oatmeal each. We then went on, when I became so feeble that myself and two more hired a Frenchman to carry us on at our own expense for thirteen miles. There we found common rations. We then went on, all very much enfeebled by reason of sickness and hardship, for four or five days until we reached Quebec.[68]

The approaching winter presented other problems as well. Few of the troops had the clothing and supplies necessary to survive the long, cold northern winter. Most of the men had no warm hats, and some simply wore handkerchiefs on their heads. Some did not even own a pair of shoes. As winter set in, Boston patriot Thomas Craig wrote, "[I] went on parade in [my] bare feet when the snow was four or five inches deep."[69] There were also no barracks and few houses available for soldiers, so crude huts were constructed of sticks and mud.

Officers' Uniforms

While the average soldier made do with what little clothing he had, Washington ordered officers to wear specific accessories so he could distinguish them from the enlisted men. Corporals were ordered to wear a green epaulet on the right shoulder, and sergeants a red one. Captains were ordered to wear yellow ribbons called cockades sewn to their hats, while subalterns, who ranked below captain, wore green cockades. Those of higher rank wore different colored sashes across their chests.

Although Washington's orders were meant to professionalize the military, officers were expected to provide their own apparel, which was often ruined in various ways. For example, John Laurens, a South Carolina officer, used his officer's sash to truss up a wounded arm, while the rain destroyed his uniform. In a letter to his father, Laurens requested that his brother James send him a new sash:

If James can purchase a broad green ribband to serve as the ensign of my office & will keep an account of what he lays out for me in this way I shall be obliged to him—my old sash rather disfigured by

Soldiers stand proud in new uniforms of the Continental Army.

the heavy rain which half drowned us on our march to the Yellow Springs, (and which by the bye spoilt me a waistcoat and breeches of white cloth and my uniform coat, clouding them with the dye washed out of my hat) served me as a sling in our retreat from Germantown & was rendered unfit for farther service.[70]

A Soldier's Weapons

Officers could survive without their proper uniforms, but all soldiers depended mightily on their three main weapons of war—pistols, muskets, and cannons. These weapons, however, were extremely inaccurate, heavy, and difficult to use. The pistol was generally only carried by officers, and had a range of about fifteen feet.

Muskets could shoot about two hundred feet and took a soldier at least fifteen seconds to reload after shooting one bullet. Rain or improper loading in the heat of battle prevented the gun from firing, so each soldier attached a short sword, or bayonet, to the barrel of the gun, so he could stab the enemy.

Cannons were the most feared weapons. They could shoot cast-iron balls that weighed from one to twenty-four pounds up to a distance of six thousand feet. These weapons were operated by teams of artillery men who, as Peterson writes, "considered themselves a class apart [because of their] specialized skill and training."[71]

Camp Equipage

All soldiers carried what was known as "camp equipage" to help them survive in the field. As Shelley reported, "The next day after I arrived at camp, they gave me a musket and bayonet, a knapsack and canteen, a cartridge box and an old rug to sleep on."[72]

Canteens often looked like small barrels made from wooden staves about nine inches long. These vessels, filled with water or diluted

Moving cannons was backbreaking work for the soldiers.

Using a Musket

The musket was the gun most used by the average soldier during the Revolutionary War. Harold L. Peterson describes fighting with a musket in *The Book of the Continental Soldier.*

"To load a musket the soldier used a cartridge, which consisted of a bullet and a load of powder wrapped in paper. First the soldier . . . bit off the end of the cartridge, poured a little powder into the [powder receptacle by the trigger], closed [it], poured the rest of the powder down the barrel and dropped the bullet still wrapped in the paper after it. Next he drew his ramrod and rammed the ball down the barrel to make sure that it was seated tightly on top of the powder where the paper of the cartridge held it in place. These bullets were always smaller than the bore of the musket so that they could be loaded quickly and easily. Thus they needed the paper to keep them from rolling out if the muzzle were pointed down.

The basic formation for infantry soldiers armed with such muskets was the line of battle. . . . [This] consisted of two ranks of men, shoulder-to-shoulder, with a line of file-closers in the rear to take the place of fallen comrades. In this formation the regiments advanced to the attack, and in it they also received the charge of the enemy. . . . The usual procedure in an attack was to advance within sure range of the enemy (some theorists recommended thirty yards), fire a volley, then charge to decide the issue with the bayonet hand-to-hand."

---

rum, often had to be shared by eight or nine men, a practice that accelerated the spread of infectious diseases.

When food rations were available, as was sometimes the case, each soldier was supposed to receive one pound of bread, a half pound of dried meat, a pint of milk, a quart of beer, and four ounces of peas or beans daily. In addition, each man was supposed to receive about one-half pound of butter per week and one pound of soap per six men. The food was issued uncooked, but the soldiers would often pick one particularly good cook among them to prepare food for a group of eight or nine men.

Cooking utensils were made from cast iron and were extremely heavy. It was the unfortunate soldier who was forced to carry such large utensils—especially when there was no food to be had. Martin writes about lugging a cook pot while retreating from the British on Long Island:

We marched . . . for the White Plains in the night. There were but three of our men present. We had our cooking utensils (at that time the most useless things in the army) to carry in our hands. They were made of cast iron and consequently heavy. I was so beat out before morning with hunger and fatigue that I could hardly move one foot before the other. I told my messmates that I *could not* carry our kettle any further. They said they *would not* carry it any further. Of what use was it? They had nothing to cook and did not want anything to cook with. . . . I could not carry it. My arms were almost dislocated. I sat [the kettle] down in the road and one of the others gave it a shove with his foot and it rolled down against the fence, and that was the last time I ever saw it. When we got through the night's march, we found our mess was not the only one that was rid of their iron bondage.[73]

War Stories

Daily life in the army was tedious and difficult, but battle posed new horrors for the Revolutionary soldier. Martin engaged the enemy many times, and many of his missions were cat-and-mouse games as small companies of men fought the British over a particularly strategic hill or a warehouse filled with barrels of flour. Martin writes about his fellow soldiers as they blundered from one skirmish to the next in the New York region: "The men were confused, being without officers to command them. I do not recollect of seeing a commissioned officer from the time I left the lines on the banks of the East River. . . . How could the men fight without officers?"[74]

Organized patrols hunted the countryside in search of the enemy who were sometimes Hessian soldiers who spoke only German. Expert marksman John McCasland wrote about one such mission in Bucks County, Pennsylvania, about sixteen miles from Philadelphia:

[On] one occasion, sixteen of us were ranging about hunting Hessians, and we suspected Hessians to be at a large and handsome mansion house. . . . We approached near the house and discovered a large Hessian standing in the yard with his gun . . . and by a unanimous vote of the company present it was agreed on that Major McCorman or myself, who were good marksmen, should shoot him. . . . We cast lots, and it fell to my lot to shoot the Hessian. I did not like to shoot a man down in cold blood. The company present knew I was a good marksman, and I concluded to break his thigh. I shot with a rifle and aimed at his hip. He had a large iron tobacco box in his breeches pocket, and I hit the box, the ball glanced, and it entered his thigh and scaled the bone of the thigh on the outside. He fell and then rose. We scaled the yard fence and surrounded the house. They saw their situation and were evidently disposed to surrender. They could not speak English, and we could not understand their language. At length one of the Hessians came out of the cellar with a large bottle of rum and advanced with it at arm's length as a flag of truce. . . . We took them prisoners and carried them to Valley Forge and delivered them up to General Washington.[75]

This sort of mission was common, but American and British soldiers also engaged in prolonged firefights. During a retreat from the British in New Jersey, Martin was pinned down by gunfire behind a battery of old timbers. He writes about this ordeal:

It was utterly impossible to lie down and get any rest or sleep on account of the mud, if the enemy's shot would have [allowed] us to do so. . . . I was in this place a fortnight [two weeks] and can say in all sincerity that I never lay down to sleep a minute in all that time.[76]

Between battles the Revolutionary soldier was forced to live in the most wretched conditions. In December 1776 soldier Joseph Woods wrote a letter to a friend describing the misery at Fort Ticonderoga in New York:

For all . . . [the] twelve or thirteen thousand men, sick and well, no more than nine hundred pair of shoes have been sent. One third at least of the poor wretches is now barefoot, and in this condition obliged to do duty. This is shocking to humanity. It cannot be viewed in any milder light than black murder. The poor creatures is now (what's left alive) laying on the cold ground, in poor thin tents, and some none at all, and many down with the pleurisy. No barracks, no hospitals to go in. . . . If you was here, your heart would melt. I paid a visit to the sick: yesterday in a small house called a hospital. The first object presented [to] my eyes, one man laying dead at the door; [then] inside two more laying dead, two living lying between them; the living with the dead had so laid for four-and-twenty hours. I went no further; this was too much to see and to much too feel, for a heart with the least tincture of humanity.[77]

Valley Forge

The situation described by Woods was repeated elsewhere, especially early in the war. The winter of 1777–1778 at Valley Forge, Pennsylvania, has gone down in history as one of the bleakest military bivouacs in history.

Washington's army was forced to retreat to the area when the British captured Philadelphia in late 1777. While British general Howe and his officers settled into the most luxurious homes in the city, the Continental Army sought winter quarters about eighteen miles northwest of Philadelphia, where they attempted to keep the British from sending their foraging parties out into the farmlands of Pennsylvania.

The *Jersey* Prison Ship

During the war the British were able to take thousands of Americans prisoner. For example, four thousand soldiers in the Continental Army were captured in New York City, and five thousand were captured when the British took Charleston, South Carolina. Many of these men were housed in despicable conditions in dungeons and abandoned buildings. One of the most infamous prisons was the ship *Jersey*. In *Recollections of the Jersey Prison Ship*, Captain Thomas Dring recalls his first day on the deck of the prison ship as a captured rebel.

"I found myself surrounded by a motley crew of wretches with tattered garments and pallid visages, who had hurried from below, for the luxury of a little fresh air. Among them, I saw one ruddy and healthful countenance, and recognized the features of one of my . . . fellow prisoners. But how different did he appear from the group around him, who had here been doomed to combat with disease and death. Men who, shrunken and decayed as they stood around him, had been, but a short time before, as strong, as healthful and as vigorous as himself. Men who had breathed the pure breezes of the ocean, or danced lightly in the flower-scented air of the meadow and the hill; and had from thence been hurried into the pent-up air of a crowded prison ship, pregnant with putrid fever, foul with deadly contagion; here to linger out the tedious and weary day, the disturbed and anxious night; to count over the days and weeks and months of a wearying and degrading captivity, unvaried but by new scenes of painful suffering, and new inflictions of remorseless cruelty: their brightest hope and their daily prayer, that death would not long delay to release them from their torments."

Men dressed as Continental Army soldiers march through the snow in this modern re-enactment of the harsh winter of 1777–1778 at Valley Forge.

As the snow began to fall, the fighting was effectively over until spring. Nonetheless the twelve thousand men in the Continental Army had to march through snow six inches deep to Valley Forge, where they needed to build a camp and defenses in the wilderness.

About two thousand huts were constructed of sticks and mud, each one large enough to hold six sleeping men. As the winter progressed, promised meat and bread supplies were never delivered. The men were forced to eat an unappetizing concoction called "firecake," made from a mixture of flour, water, and ashes from a fire, baked on the back of a metal shovel. Martin describes the misery:

The army was now not only starved but naked. The greatest part were not only shirtless and barefoot, but destitute of all other clothing, especially blankets. I procured a small piece of raw cowhide and made myself a pair of moccasins which kept my feet . . . from the frozen ground, although, as I well remember, the hard edges so galled my ankles . . . that it was with much difficulty and pain that I could wear them. . . . But the only alternative I had was to . . . go barefoot, as hundreds of my companions had to, till they might be tracked by their blood upon the rough frozen ground. But hunger, nakedness and sore shins were not the only difficulties

Lives of Revolutionary Soldiers

we had at this time to encounter; we had hard duty to perform and little or no strength to perform it with.[78]

Throughout the winter the men slept on lice-infested straw beds while their fingers, toes, arms, and legs blackened from frostbite. Washington continually wrote a series of angry letters to Congress begging for money and supplies and warning of mutiny.

The morale of the troops was lifted somewhat when Baron Friedrich von Stuben, a Prussian general, was brought in to drill the troops in their winter camp. Although he spoke no English, von Stuben taught the men how to handle their muskets, march with the discipline of the European regiment, and act like professional soldiers. With intense daily training the men gained renewed confidence in themselves and their cause. Although about four thousand men, or one-third of the soldiers, perished that winter at Valley Forge, when spring came, the Continental Army had renewed purpose.

Although the war would last another five years, Valley Forge was a turning point. When Washington's troops marched into Philadelphia that spring, they had overcome the odds and beaten hardship and adversity. Victory appeared to be within reach.

Women in the Revolution

Although soldiers suffered the greatest hardship during the war, their mothers, wives, and daughters also made extreme sacrifices for the Revolution. With nearly nine out of ten Americans living in rural areas, most women were far from the battle lines. But while the men were serving in the military, it was the women who were left in charge of running farm households and struggling for survival.

Life was uncertain—and often short—in the eighteenth century, especially during the Revolution. Women were married by the time they were eighteen, and marriage was an arrangement between families, not between young men and women. The romantic desires of the young were sometimes taken into account, but usually, girls were expected to marry boys who would improve the family's wealth or social position.

With little access to birth control, women usually became pregnant soon after marriage, and often spent much of their lives carrying or nursing babies. In *To Be Useful to the World,* Joan R. Gundersen writes about this situation as it affected a woman named Elizabeth Porter in Virginia: "After 24 years of marriage, 10 pregnancies, and 8 living children, the 43-year-old Elizabeth finally finished bearing children. Her experience . . . was common among native-born Chesapeake women in the eighteenth century."[79]

Pregnant women were expected to perform their daily chores until it was time to give birth. Babies were delivered at home, in bed.

The mother was often surrounded by the other females in the family and aided by an experienced older woman known as a midwife. Doctors were rarely present, and about 25 percent of colonial women died from complications of childbirth. Due to diseases, infant mortality was also high, and nearly 50 percent of children died before they reached the age of sixteen.

Feeding Families

In war and in peace life was anything but easy for rural farm families, who continually battled nature to clear land, plant crops, and wrest a living from the soil. Women did more than cook and clean for their large families. They also milked cows, carried water, made soap, butchered livestock, smoked and preserved meat, and acted as the family doctor.

Cooking for large families was an arduous task in the days before modern appliances. Women prepared family meals over large open fireplaces found in every kitchen. Children were enlisted to keep the fire burning day and night, and coals were raked under individual pots to regulate heat. Each fireplace had a long metal pole thrust across it upon which cast-iron pots were suspended by pot hooks. Large pots—weighing up to forty pounds when full—were used for boiling liquids, rendering fat, simmering soups and stews, and curing meats.

Frying was done in large, long-handled, three-legged, cast-iron frying pans placed

*A colonial kitchen bustles
with activity.*

directly over the coals. Maneuvering these heavy utensils filled with boiling liquids and hot foods was dangerous. Thousands of women were severely burned or even killed in cooking accidents, especially when long dresses, petticoats, or aprons caught fire.

Vegetable gardens were particularly important to rural survival, and women harvested a cornucopia of fresh foods for their families, including apples, asparagus, beans, pears, peas, potatoes, radishes, raspberries, and strawberries. What was not eaten fresh was preserved as pickles, jams, and jellies in clay jars. And if a family had cows, goats, or sheep, women churned butter and made cheese. In the 1975 *National Geographic* article "Patriots in Petticoats," Lonnelle Aikman describes how this way of life naturally helped women during the Revolution:

> Schooled in the vast untamed land of hardships and hazards, the women of Colonial America were conditioned to independence and initiative. From Canada's forest-shadowed St. Lawrence Valley to the southern seaports of the Atlantic and westward to the wild frontier of the Indi-

ans, they made homes with whatever came handy.

Up at dawn, growing and preparing their own foods, spinning, making their own clothing, and nursing the sick with medicines from herb gardens and nature's field-and-forest apothecaries, most of them found that a woman's work, indeed, was never done.

At the same time they were "borning" children with the regularity of the seasons. And where Indians raided or outlaws attacked, they were capable of grabbing the nearest weapon and defending their families. No wonder many women were ready to give up imported comforts and luxuries rather than submit to oppressive British taxation.

Better, they said, to wear plain homespun dresses than to flaunt gaudy, expensive ones from Europe. As for British tea, there were plenty of native substitutes—sage, currant, strawberry, loosestrife, or plantain leaves—which they brewed and served as Liberty Tea.[80]

Life in the City

It was not only fiercely independent country women who supported the Revolution. Eighteenth-century cities also forced women to deal with hardship and learn to survive through strength and independent action.

In the uncertain years before the war tens of thousands of immigrants poured into American cities. About 25 percent of those newcomers were women. While some traveled with husbands or families, many were alone, attracted by employment opportunities unavailable in their native lands. These women—many in their late teens or early twenties—came from Ireland, Scotland, England, Germany, Switzerland, France, Italy, or Greece to work as gardeners, maids, washwomen, cooks, and servants in the homes of well-to-do citizens.

Women new to the colonies faced special hardships. Although employment was readily available, women's wages were lower than those of men, and it was difficult for them to improve their situation because they were not allowed to own property or vote. Gundersen describes other difficulties faced by women: "Far removed from the protection of family and friends, women were at greater risk than men of sexual and physical abuse. Harsh masters raped, whipped, or starved servants; some women bartered sexual access for better treatment."[81]

Married women whose husbands were artisans, tradesmen, or merchants had an easier time than the newly arrived immigrants. Like rural women, they spent most of their lives pregnant, nursing babies, and taking care of children. But it was common for middle-class women to hire nurses, nannies, or servants to help them with their daily chores.

Many women spent their time shopping for family necessities, and clothing stores were particularly prevalent, with many specializing in women's clothes, perfumes, accessories, and shoes. Fashionable hairstyles were also popular, and hairdressers specialized in cutting hair and grooming the extravagant wigs popular among the wealthy classes.

Women in the wealthy classes wore the most fashionable styles and prided themselves on their extravagant powdered wigs.

One of the most famous women of the American Revolution is Betsy Ross, who is widely credited with sewing the first American flag. Her biography is posted on the Betsy Ross: Her Life website.

"Elizabeth Griscom—also called Betsy . . . was born on January 1, 1752. . . . Betsy went to a Friends [Quaker] public school. . . . After completing her schooling, Betsy's father apprenticed her to a local upholsterer . . . [who] performed all manner of sewing jobs, including flag-making. It was at her job that Betsy fell in love with another apprentice, John Ross, who was the son of an Episcopal assistant rector at Christ Church.

Quakers frowned on inter-denominational marriages. The penalty for such unions was severe—the guilty party being 'read out' [which] meant being cut off emotionally and economically from both family and [Quaker] meeting house. . . . On a November night in 1773, 21-year-old Betsy eloped with John Ross. . . . Her wedding caused an irrevocable split from her family. . . .

Less than two years after their nuptials, the couple started their own upholstery business. . . . [On] Sundays one could now find Betsy at Christ Church . . . with her husband. Some Sundays would find George Washington, America's new commander in chief, sitting in an adjacent pew.

Betsy and John Ross keenly felt the impact of the war. . . . John joined the Pennsylvania militia. While guarding an ammunition cache . . . Ross was mortally wounded in an explosion. Though his young wife tried to nurse him back to health he died. . . .

In late May or early June of 1776, according to Betsy's telling, she had that fateful meeting with the Committee of Three: George Washington, George Ross, and Robert Morris, which led to the sewing of the first flag. . . . Betsy died on January 30, 1836, at the age of 84."

George Washington and members of Congress consult with Betsy Ross on the design of the first American flag.

Not all middle-class women spent their time shopping. Ambitious women or those who were widowed often ran their own businesses. And a large percentage of middle-class women helped their husbands run the family business. A good example is Benjamin Franklin's wife, Deborah, who helped her husband run his print shop. According to Gundersen,

> Deborah managed the accounts, folded and stitched pamphlets, tended shop, purchased rags for paper making. Under her management the print shop expanded beyond stationery to general merchandise. After Benjamin's appointment as postmaster general for the colonies, Deborah oversaw the operations as well, even when pregnant with Sally.[82]

While Deborah took part in her husband's printing business, Mary Katherine Goddard became the first female publisher in the colonies when she began the *Providence Gazette* in Rhode Island in 1762. In January 1777, Goddard made her place in history when she issued the first printed copy of the Declaration of Independence to include the signers' names.

Deborah Franklin and Mary Katherine Goddard were only two of many working women in the eighteenth century. In Philadelphia, about 15 percent of retail shops were run by women, and about two out of ten tavern keepers were women. Throughout the colonies women were in charge of coffeehouses, restaurants, boardinghouses, inns, and other businesses. In Boston women made saddles, knives, beer, soap, bread, clothes, and even iron nails and horseshoes. In the southern colonies where craft workers were scarce, women performed jobs traditionally held by men, working as gunsmiths, blacksmiths, shipwrights, tanners, shoemakers, and furniture makers.

Retail shops, like this shoemaker's establishment, employed women.

Revolutionary Support and Sacrifice

Whether they worked at home or in a business environment, women were called on to make the greatest sacrifices as the protests against British policies began in the 1760s. When the colonists called for a boycott on all British imported goods, women had to find substitutes for British teas, cloth, and other luxuries from abroad. This caused a massive clothing shortage in the colonies—one that women were called upon to solve. Raphael explains,

> During the peak of resistance to the hated Townshend duties of 1767, some visionary patriots seized upon an idea: why not commandeer the traditional New England "spinning bee" for political use? Customarily, a number of female churchgoers would gather from time to time at the house of their minister to spin for his personal wardrobe; after they finished [the] work of the day, they would listen to his sermon. These special events helped alleviate isolation and monotony as participating women conveniently combined work, socializing, and religion. Starting in 1768 and peaking in 1769, patriotic newspapers invested the spinning bees with new meaning. . . . They became "ideological showcases" of the nonimportation movement as women spun not only for their preachers but for the good of their country. Spinning bees, according to their promoters, served . . . to demonstrate that women could become patriots without departing from traditional concepts of femininity.[83]

Many women openly supported the patriot cause in other ways and were willing to

Clothing for the Revolution

As with many other products, clothing was a source of contention between the colonials and their British rulers. In *To Be Useful to the World,* Joan R. Gundersen explains how women reacted to the nonimportation of cloth on the eve of the Revolution.

"The movement for independence politicized women's sewing and cloth production. The purchase of imported cloth added to colonial indebtedness and dependence on Britain. Spinning bees became public rituals demonstrating colonial self-sufficiency and firmness as boycotts of imported goods became the main form of resistance to imperial taxation. Used earlier to publicize efforts to set up manufactories to employ the poor, the ritual of a public spinning now merged with Revolutionary fervor. Elite women and girls demonstrated their patriotism by participating in public spinning bees. Urban public spinnings could involve 40–100 young women at a time and attract 600 spectators. From 1768 to 1770 there were at least 46 such bees (30 in 1769 alone), involving 1,644 women. Nearly three-quarters were held at ministers' homes. Such public events were less about production (often the work was donated to clergy or charities) than about demonstrating solidarity. The women arrived wearing homespun [clothes], and had colonial-grown refreshments and herbal (not imported) tea. Home spinning gained new meaning."

sacrifice their comfort and safety in order to fight British rule. From the beginning of the troubles women organized meeting groups and signed petitions to protest British policies. In 1766 the Daughters of Liberty was organized as a female auxiliary to the tax-defying Sons of Liberty. In 1770 more than three hundred Boston women stated that they would not drink any more tea so that they might "save this abused Country from Ruin and Slavery."[84] And in 1774 fifty-one women in Edenton, North Carolina, risked arrest by sending a petition condemning tea taxes to Parliament in London.

Patriot women were proud of their ability to participate in political life. One such woman was Eliza Wilkinson from South Carolina, who wrote a letter about her meeting group, saying,

> [Never] were greater politicians than the several knots of ladies, who meet together. All trifling discourse of fashions, and such low little chat was thrown by, and we commenced [to be] perfect statesmen. Indeed, I don't know but if we had taken a little pains, we should have been qualified for prime ministers, so well could we discuss several important matters at hand.[85]

Terrifying Ordeals

When the shooting started, tens of thousands of men left their farms and villages to join the army. Farm women, who were already burdened with an unending series of chores, were forced to take over men's work as well, plowing fields, planting crops, pulling weeds, and harvesting in the fall. They also had to tend to livestock, repair their homes and farm buildings, mend fences, cut wood for the fireplace,

A Thousand Things That Must Be Done

In 1775 Temperance Smith from Sharon, Connecticut, described her life after her husband went off to fight the British. The pages of her diary were reprinted in *A People's History of the American Revolution* by Ray Raphael.

"When the [actions] of the Mother Country [Britain] had rendered it impossible for any but the wealthiest to import anything to eat or wear, and all had to be raised and manufactured at home, from bread stuffs, sugar and rum to the linen and woollen for our clothes and bedding, you may well imagine that my duties were not light, though I can say for myself that I never complained, even in my inmost thoughts. . . .

To tell the truth, I had no leisure for murmuring. I rose with the sun and all through the long day I had no time for aught but my work. So much did it press upon me that I could scarcely divert my thoughts from its demands, even during the family prayers, which thing both amazed and displeased me, for during that hour, at least, I should have been sending all my thoughts to heaven for the safety of my beloved husband and the salvation of our hapless country. Instead of which I was often wondering whether Polly had remembered to set the sponge for the bread, or to put water on the leach tub, or to turn the cloth in the dying vat, or whether wool had been carded for Betsey to start her spinning wheel in the morning, or Billy had chopped light wood enough for the kindling, or dry hard wood enough to heat the big oven, or whether some other thing had not been forgotten of the thousand that must be done without fail, or else there would be a disagreeable hitch in the housekeeping."

and keep tools in good repair. Although many women were helped by their children, it was extremely burdensome for most.

The situation was worse still for those who lived near armies on the march. Whether Continental or British, the soldiers—many of whom were on the brink of starvation—appropriated grain, cattle, and the produce from fields and vegetable gardens, leaving women and their families to starve long after the hordes had moved on. As Post writes, "Were I to undertake to relate the injuries, insults, horrors, and sufferings [we] are subject to, I should never finish the story."[86]

Finding enough food was a large problem, and with the men gone, the women were also left to defend themselves as the social order crumbled into chaos. In the countryside thieves and highwaymen took advantage of isolated women—many of whom were taking care of their aged parents. Post describes one terrifying event:

The robbers, on entering the house of [Mrs.] Willis, were so exasperated at finding no booty, that they tied the hands of all the family behind them. . . .

They dragged the wife of Mr. Willis by the hair about the house, and then left them, telling them that they had set fire to the house, which was true, as they saw the flames kindling and curling up the wooden jamb beside the fireplace. Their hands all tied! . . . A young woman named Phebe Powell, by dint of the most powerful efforts, at length loosened one of her hands and ran to extinguish the flames, which she succeeded in doing before releasing the rest from their thongs![87]

In addition to the bandits that Post sometimes derisively called "Cow Boys," the countryside was also haunted by "runners," or spies from British camps, who frightened men, women, and children wherever they operated. According to Post,

"Runners" . . . are generally seen lurking about at twilight, spying points most favorable for attack. . . . Sometimes they will stop, and inquire the way to some place; suddenly disappearing, they are unexpectedly seen again in the edge of the wood, or from behind a hay-stack in the field, peering about, terrifying every body, above all women and children.[88]

Home invasions were also committed by British soldiers intent on rooting out "women rebels." Wilkinson writes of redcoats riding up to her house in a thunder of horses' hooves, cursing loudly and crashing through the door with pistols and swords drawn. Finding only three terrified women, the men broke into trunks and "plundered the house of every thing they thought valuable or worth taking."[89] Wilkinson begged the men in vain to leave her at least one dress, since clothing was extremely difficult to find during the wartime shortages. Instead, the men bent over to steal the gold buckles from the shoes on her feet. The redcoats then turned to the other women in the house, as Wilkinson writes:

[They] took my sister's ear-rings from her ears; hers, and Miss Samuells's buckles; they demanded her ring from her finger; she pleaded for it, told them it was her wedding ring, and begged they'd let her keep it; but they still demanded it, and, presenting a pistol at her, swore if she did not deliver it immediately, they'd fire. She gave it to them, and after bundling up all their booty, they mounted their horses.

Women and children were the targets of home invasions by British soldiers.
Here, the British question a small boy.

But such despicable figures! Each wretch's bosom stuffed so full they appeared to be all afflicted with some [disease]. . . .

The whole world appeared to me as a theater, where nothing was acted but cruelty, bloodshed, and oppression; where neither age nor sex escaped the horrors of injustice and violence; where the lives and property of the innocent and inoffensive were in continual danger, and the lawless power ranged at large. . . .

[After the invasion, we] could neither eat, drink, nor sleep in peace; for as we lay in our clothes every night, we could not enjoy the little sleep we got. The least noise alarmed us; up we would jump, expecting every moment to hear them demand admittance. In short, our nights were wearisome and painful; our days spent in anxiety and melancholy.[90]

To add to the pain, many women missed their husbands and constantly worried about the well-being of the men so far away. Since letters were the only means of communication —and those took weeks or months to be delivered—married women spent many of their waking hours in a state of anxiety, not knowing if their soldier husbands were dead or alive. As Post writes,

Days of agony and nights of tears are my experience; the agony of suspense, the tears of widowhood! In imagination I have no longer a husband! He is slain on the field of battle, of which no tidings have come; or the victim of neglected wounds and disease, he is in the hands of the enemy. If alive and at liberty, we surely should long ago have heard from him. How *can* I endure it? Oh, God endue [provide] me with patience, or I sink![91]

Fighting Back

While rural women like Post suffered alone, some women banded together—and resorted to violence—to improve their situation. In 1777, when a merchant in Poughkeepsie, New York, hoarded tea to drive up its price, twenty-two women rioted, broke into his shop, and stole his tea. In Massachusetts, the same situation arose when a shop owner tried to stockpile coffee. Abigail Adams wrote of the melee:

An eminent, wealthy, stingy merchant (also a bachelor) had a hogshead of coffee in his store, which he refused to sell . . . under six shillings per pound. A number of Females, some say a hundred, some say more, assembled with a cart and trunks, marched down to the [warehouse] and demanded the keys, which he refused to deliver. Upon which one of them seized him by his Neck and tossed him into the cart. Upon his finding no quarter, he delivered the keys when they tipped up the cart and discharged him; they opened the Warehouse, hoisted out the Coffee themselves, put it into the trunks and drove off. . . . A large concourse of men stood amazed silent Spectators.[92]

Abigail Adams often sternly prodded her husband, John Adams, to consider the rights of women.

Other women laid their lives on the line to resist the British. In New York, Catherine Van Rennsaelear Schuyler, the mother of fourteen children, burned her family's corn crop in the field so that approaching British troops could not harvest the ripened ears. Her action inspired her neighbors to do the same. In South Carolina, Anne Kennedy picked up her blunderbuss and began shooting at redcoats who were stealing her crops. Although she suffered a minor wound, her attack succeeded in driving off the British soldiers. Nancy Hart of Georgia also picked up her weapon to defend her property against a group of Loyalists who overran her cabin; she shot and killed one and held the rest at gunpoint until help arrived.

Some female patriots, especially young women, were able to pass British sentries unnoticed and deliver important military messages. In 1777 sixteen-year-old Sybil Ludington of Connecticut rode her horse forty miles from town to town calling up militiamen after the British destroyed a supply cache in Danbury. Deborah Champion rode for two days to carry military intelligence to George Washington. In Virginia another sixteen-year-old, Susanna Bolling, rode alone through the night, crossing the Appomattox River to warn American allies of British troops preparing to attack. These young women faced grave dangers if caught; they could have been jailed and executed for treason.

Women also acted as spies, sometimes at work, eavesdropping on British soldiers in taverns and boardinghouses. As Aikman writes, "In North Carolina . . . Martha Bell . . . rode the countryside picking up hints of British strength to aid Gen. Nathaniel Green's campaign against Lord Cornwallis."[93]

Those unable to act as messengers or spies provided desperately needed supplies to the patriots. When the fighting began,

Patriots dismantle a statue of King George III. Hundreds of statues of the monarch were destroyed and the metal they contained melted down and formed into musket balls by the women of the Revolution.

hundreds of metal statues of the British king George III that stood on public squares were melted down and turned into musket balls by women; more than forty-two thousand were forged from one statue in Bowling Green, New York, alone. Women also melted down jewelry, pewter dishes, and other personal goods for the cause. One patriot in Boston, "Handy Betty the Blacksmith," was known for her metalworking skill, repairing weapons and making bullets for militiamen.

Other women recycled clothing for the soldiers. When Washington's ill-equipped Continental Army froze at Valley Forge during the terrible winter of 1777–1778, Mary Frazier of Chester County took it upon herself to find stockings and blankets for the patriots, many of whom were dying of exposure. According to Sarah Frazier, her granddaughter,

[Mary rode her horse] day after day collecting from neighbors and friends far and near, whatever they could spare for the comfort of the destitute soldiers, the blankets, and yarn, and half worn clothing thus obtained she brought to her own house, where they would be patched, and darned, and made wearable and comfortable, the stockings newly footed, or new ones knit, adding what clothing she could give of her own. She often sat up half the night, sometimes all, to get clothing ready. Then with it, and whatever could be obtained for food, she would have packed on her horse and set out on her cold lonely journey to the camp—which she went to repeatedly during the winter.[94]

Camp Followers

While farm women stayed home to work and defend their property, thousands of other women had little in the way of resources and were forced to become "camp followers" who traveled side-by-side with the soldiers. These women might have been unemployed widows simply hired as cooks and nurses. Others were women whose husbands were in the military who had no other means of support.

Most camp followers had few other options in life, traveling with the military for meager pay, a few scraps of meat, or possibly the love of a soldier. A few wealthy women, however, such as George Washington's wife, Martha, traveled with the army to advise and support their husbands. Aikman describes the travels of Mrs. Washington:

Seated in the family coach . . . surrounded by hams, jellies, and other plantation goodies to augment lean camp fare, she jolted over rough roads for days at a time to reach the headquarters of the Rebel commander and his troops.

Beginning with Cambridge, from which she watched the British evacuate Boston, she was with the general in New York City, Morristown [New Jersey], Valley Forge, and Middlebrook [New Jersey]. . . .

To reach [Valley Forge in February 1778,] she and her military escort had clattered past hundreds of hand-hewn log huts in which some 11,000 hungry, near naked soldiers chanted hopelessly from time to time, "No meat, no clothes, no pay, no rum."[95]

Of course most camp followers did not have the luxuries afforded the commanding general's wife. In fact they performed some of the most difficult and dirty jobs, cleaning endless piles of filthy clothes stained with blood, sweat, and dirt, or cooking for hundreds of often ungrateful men. During combat camp followers dodged bullets and enemy soldiers to carry messages and supplies between the lines. In return these women were given little pay or respect. They were also last in line when food, blankets, and other necessities were handed out.

"Beasts of Burthen"

Despite the miserable conditions, the military high command looked on the camp followers as a necessary evil, since it was a commonly held belief that if men could not bring their wives and families along with them on their military missions, many soldiers would desert and simply return home.

Washington, however, believed that the presence of camp followers slowed his army's progress, writing in 1777, "In the present marching state of the army . . . the multitude of women in particular, especially those who are pregnant, or have children, are a clog upon every movement."[96]

The commander was also embarrassed by the ragtag assemblage of women and children that rode along in military wagons with his troops. He issued orders that women were to be forbidden to ride in the wagons and were to march to the rear with the baggage. These orders were repeatedly ignored by some men who refused to make their wives march. Finally, after a half-dozen decrees, the frustrated Washington wrote, "[The] pernicious practice of suffering [allowing] the women to encumber the Waggons still continues notwithstanding every former prohibition."[97]

On the British side there were even greater numbers of camp followers, possibly because the British had captured several major cities. Whatever the reason, for every four British soldiers, there was one camp follower. The Americans had less than half that many. One British general wrote about his troops, "Their number of women and the quantity of baggage is astonishing."[98]

In *Women Camp Followers of the American Revolution*, Walter Hart Blumenthal details the numbers of women among British and Hessian troops in 1781 near the end of the war: There was "a grand total of 23,489 men, 3,615 women, 4,127 children. The British regiments comprise 9,686 men and 2,173 women, the Germanic regiments 10,251 men and 679 women, the civil departments (Quartermaster, Commissary, Engineer, Hospital, Barrack, Boatmen personnel) 3,512 men and 763 women."[99]

Apparently the British camp followers were even more miserable than their American counterparts. Their appalling condition was recorded by patriot Hannah Winthrop, who wrote,

I never had the least Idea that the Creation produced such a sordid set of creatures in human Figure—poor, dirty, emaciated . . . women who seem to be the beasts of burthen, having a bushel basket on their back, by which they were bent double, the contents seem to be Pots and Kettles. . . . [Some carry] very young infants who were born on the road, the women [had] bare feet, cloathed in dirty rags, such effluvia [odorous fumes] filld the air while they were passing . . . I should have been apprehensive of being contaminated by them.[100]

In addition to their other hardships camp followers were often in the line of fire. Many died from battle wounds, but some learned to fight with bravery and honor. Twenty-five-year-old Margaret Cochran Corbin was a camp follower who accompanied her husband, John, to the battle at Fort Washington in New York. "Molly," as she was known, was helping her husband swab out the cannon barrel and ram ammunition down the neck when John was shot dead. Corbin took his battle station under intense fire and continued to load and fire the cannon by herself. She received a blast of buckshot in the breast, shoulder, and jaw.

Corbin survived but was never able to use her left arm again. The Americans lost the battle, but the wounded, such as Corbin, were returned to the Continental Army. In 1779 Margaret Cochran Corbin became the first

Margaret Cochran Corbin, pictured here swabbing out a cannon barrel, was the first woman in U.S. history to receive a disabled soldier's military pension.

woman in U.S. history to receive a disabled soldiers' military pension, receiving a monthly stipend and an annual allotment for clothing.

"Remember the Ladies"

The average woman was forced to make many unpleasant choices during the war, but those in the upper class often had the luxury of exploring Revolutionary promises of freedom, liberty, and full representation in the government. In fact the Revolution produced something of an eighteenth-century women's liberation movement among the educated classes.

Abigail Adams, the wife of second president John Adams, often prodded her husband to remember women's rights. In March 1776,

even before the Declaration of Independence was signed, Adams wrote her husband,

> I long to hear that you have declared an independency—and by the way in the new Code of Laws which I suppose it will be necessary for you to make I desire you would Remember the Ladies, and be more generous and favourable to them than your ancestors. Do not put such unlimited power in the hands of the Husbands. Remember all Men would be tyrants if they could. If [particular] care and attention is not paid to the Ladies we are determined to foment a Rebellion, and will not hold ourselves bound by any Laws in which we have no voice, or Representation.[101]

The sentiments expressed by Abigail Adams were found elsewhere as well, and as the protests spread across the land, thousands of women were swept up in the Revolutionary excitement of the day. Many found this discourse liberating, as Wilkinson writes:

I do not love to meddle with political matters; the men say we had no business with them, it is not our sphere! . . . I won't have that thought, that because we're the weaker sex as to *bodily* strength . . . we are capable of nothing more than minding the dairy, visiting the poultry-house, and all such domestic concerns; our thoughts can soar aloft, we can form conceptions of things of higher nature; we have as just a sense of honor, glory, and the greater actions, as these "Lords of Creation." . . . They won't even allow us the liberty of thought, and that is all I want. I would not wish that we should meddle in what is unbecoming . . . [behavior], but surely we may have sense enough to give our opinions . . . [on] such actions as we may approve or disapprove; without being reminded of our spinning and household affairs as the only matters we are capable of thinking or speaking of with justness or propriety. I won't allow it, positively won't.[102]

Women Go to War

Not all soldiers who fought in the Revolution were men according to the Women Soldiers in the American Revolutionary War website.

"In October of 1778 Deborah Samson of Plymouth Massachusetts disguised herself as a young man and presented herself to the American army as a willing volunteer to oppose the common enemy. She enlisted for the whole term of the war as Robert Shirtliffe. . . .

For three years she served in various duties and was wounded twice—the first time by a sword cut on the side of the head and four months later she was shot through the shoulder. Her sexual identity went undetected until she came down with a brain fever. . . . The attending physician . . . discovered her charade, but said nothing. Instead he had her taken to his own home where she would receive better care. When her health was restored . . . an order was issued for Robert Shirtliffe to carry a letter to General Washington [in Philadelphia]. . . .

When the order came . . . she knew that her deception was over. She presented herself at the headquarters of Washington, trembling with dread and uncertainty. General Washington, to spare her embarrassment, said nothing. Instead he sent her with an aide to have some refreshments, then summoned her back. In silence Washington handed Deborah Samson a discharge from the service, a note with some words of advice, and a sum of money sufficient to bear her expenses home.

After the war Deborah Samson married Benjamin Gannett of Sharon and they had three children. During George Washington's presidency she received a letter inviting Robert Shirtliffe, or rather Mrs. Gannett, to visit Washington. During her stay at the capital a bill was passed granting her a pension, in addition to certain lands, which she was to receive as an acknowledgment for her services to the country in a military capacity as a Revolutionary Soldier."

Emboldened by such thoughts, many women took it upon themselves to challenge the British who occupied their towns. Their rebelliousness helped lower the morale of the redcoats. In 1781, after the war had slogged on for six years, one British soldier in Charleston, South Carolina, wrote,

Even in their dress the females seem to bid us defiance. . . . [They] take care to have [on] their breasts . . . and even on their shoes something that resembles their flag of the thirteen stripes. An officer told Lord Cornwallis [the commander of the British troops in America] . . . that he believed if he had destroyed all the men in North America, we should have enough to do to conquer the women." [103]

Overall, American women aided the Revolutionary victory in thousands of ways. Although their contribution was largely ignored at the time, in the last few decades researchers have discovered diaries, memoirs, and other records and have brought to light the role of patriot women in American history. But for each heroic deed that has been revealed, thousands remain anonymous, buried by the passage of time. Despite this fact, from the early tax revolts to the first shots fired at Lexington to the final battles of Yorktown, America's founding mothers made an invaluable contribution to the Revolution.

CHAPTER 5

Black Americans, Free and Slave

Women patriots fought for independence but were denied the right to vote and often the right to own property. Although they faced discrimination in daily life, they at least had the right to exercise free will. This was not the case for most African Americans during the American Revolution.

Black Americans took part in nearly every phase of the Revolution. They protested in the streets, petitioned government officials, and performed invaluable tasks for the military. About five thousand African Americans fought on the front lines on the patriot side, and thousands more served with the British. Unfortunately most black Americans who served were slaves who could not read or write. As a result there are few firsthand written records of their experiences. Most of the information available to historians was written by slave owners, government officials, and white military officers.

Black Americans fought on the patriot side at the Battle of Bunker Hill.

"Life, Liberty, and the Pursuit of Happiness"

Many black patriots were inspired to action by Thomas Jefferson's proclamation in the Declaration of Independence that "all men are created equal, they are endowed by their Creator with certain unalienable Rights, that among these are Life, Liberty, and the pursuit of Happiness." The author of these words, however, owned 187 slaves at the time the document was written, and black Americans in the eighteenth century had no such guarantee of rights.

The first black slaves had been brought to North America in 1619 when a Dutch ship deposited about twenty captured Africans at the English settlement of Jamestown, Virginia. On the eve of the Revolutionary War in 1775, there were fifty thousand slaves in the northern colonies, and they were often advertised for sale in Boston newspapers through notices like these: "To be sold, a tall, likely, straight-limbed negro of twenty-four"; "a likely negro boy of seven"; "a negro wench about nine years old"; "a negro woman with a fine child three months old"; "two negro girls of sixteen for sale cheap."[104]

The situation was similar in the South, where more than 430,000 people lived in slavery, nearly 200,000 in Virginia alone. In addition almost 4,000 kidnapped Africans were imported to that one colony every year. And during the Revolution, when there was a major breakdown of law and order, even free northern blacks, such as those in New York, were occasionally abducted by slave traders and sold in the South. As Post writes,

A new source of trouble has appeared . . . kidnapping negroes [*sic*] . . . The ruffians come in sloops from the Delaware and Maryland country, and landing on the island in the night, they steal the poor crea-

tures while asleep, after the labor of cutting the salt meadowgrass. . . . When they get them away, they sell them at the South.

A week since, while the men were at work, four persons, in broad day, their faces blackened, and dressed like negroes, appeared suddenly, each armed with a gun, and before the others could come to the rescue, a man and a boy were forcibly taken, put in a boat, and rowed off to a cutter out at sea. On the deck the villains could be seen putting chains on the poor creatures. I tremble at the thought of the future![105]

Northern blacks were treated slightly better than those in the southern colonies, where slaves greatly outnumbered whites. In South Carolina, for instance, 80 percent of the population consisted of black slaves. Despite this fact large plantations with hundreds of slaves were uncommon. Instead, about half of southern planters owned five slaves or fewer, and many other families held ten or twenty slaves.

Free blacks, while slightly more common in the North, made up a tiny percentage of the total African American population in the eighteenth century. In Maryland, for instance, there were only about eighteen hundred free blacks in a population of around fifty thousand slaves. And those who were free were mostly people of mixed racial heritage, people unable to work because of infirmities, or people too old to labor on plantations. A population of young, healthy free blacks was almost nonexistent.

With nearly one in four Americans laboring as slaves, the success and prosperity of the colonies in the last third of the eighteenth century was inextricably tied to unpaid African American labor. Nearly every aspect of

The Triangular Trade

Although slavery was most prevalent in the South, northern merchants contributed significantly by participating in what was known as the triangular trade route. Merchants who specialized in the notorious triangular route shipped rum, gunpowder, and guns produced in New England to Africa, where these goods were exchanged for slaves. The slaves were transported on the infamous "Middle Passage" to the West Indies, where the survivors were exchanged at a handsome profit for sugar and molasses, which was carried back to New England and turned into rum.

The rum trade was highly profitable, and grew more so every year. In 1771, for example, Philadelphia distilleries exported about 200,000 gallons of rum. Two years later, that number grew almost 40 percent to 278,000 gallons. These astounding production increases were matched by distilleries in New York City, Baltimore, and elsewhere.

The rum, in turn, brought an ever-increasing number of slaves to the New World. Between 1709 and 1800, merchants in the tiny colony of Rhode Island alone sponsored more than eight hundred triangular slaving voyages to Africa, carrying more than one hundred thousand kidnapped Africans from their homeland to the New World. Although some groups, especially Pennsylvania Quakers, abhorred the slave trade, little was done to stop it.

During the "Middle Passage," sick or rebellious slaves were sometimes thrown overboard to drown.

southern agriculture involved slavery. Blacks constructed roads, built plantations, and planted and harvested crops. They worked as domestic servants, cooking, serving, cleaning, gardening, tending children, and performing general housework. The duties of kitchen slaves included butchering animals, brewing beer, smoking meat, and pickling vegetables. Blacks also labored as artisans, tanning leather, making saddles and harnesses, working iron, building furniture, casting pottery, tailoring clothes, and performing hundreds of other tasks.

In return blacks were treated as the lowest members of society. These conditions were described in a 1762 pamphlet by John Woolman, one of the founders of the Quaker abolitionist, or antislavery, movement:

Placing on Men the ignominious Title, SLAVE, dressing them in uncomely Garments, keeping them to servile Labour, in which they are often dirty. . . . They have neither Honours, Riches . . . nor Power; their Dress coarse, and often ragged; their Employ Drudgery, and much in the Dirt: they have little or nothing at Command; but must wait upon and work for others to obtain the Necessaries of Life.[106]

Slaves suffered further degradation. They were bought and sold like cattle at public auctions in nearly every colonial city. Husbands and wives were separated, and children were taken from their parents.

On the farms and plantations, eighteenth-century slaves generally lived under dreadful

A public slave auction in Richmond, Virginia, in the 1850s. Auctions at the time of the Revolution were much the same.

Slaves and slave quarters in South Carolina in 1859.

conditions. Archaeologists have unearthed slave quarters in South Carolina and describe the shelters on the website titled "The Lives of African-American Slaves in Carolina During the 18th Century":

> [Eighteenth-] century slaves often lived in minimal huts built of upright poles set in a trench and covered in clay. The roofs were probably covered in palmetto fronds or other thatch.
>
> Archaeologists call these houses "wall-trench structures" and they were used at least up to the American Revolution. Most had no fireplaces and they were built with earthen floors. The buildings range from about 13 feet in length and only 9 feet in width up to about 21 feet in length and around 14 feet in width. There were only a few windows and these were all open, with perhaps only a shutter to close out the bad weather.
>
> These mudwall, thatched wall-trench buildings had relatively short lifespans, perhaps only ten years or so. They were quickly attacked by termites and other pests. The wet Southern climate eroded the clay used to plaster the walls. The houses were probably very cold in the winter and hot in the summer. Consequently, most activities took place outside and the structures were used primarily during bad weather.[107]

Although the small huts were primitive, they were the only place of refuge for slaves, who worked from sunup to sundown under grueling conditions. On large plantations slaves worked under the gang system, in which often brutal overseers used whips, chains, and guns to force labor. Children were taken from their mothers and put to work when only five years old. Women were often raped, and torturing and murdering slaves was legal. Many slaves were fed only the minimal amount of calories necessary to maintain performance. As one slave said, "we have been fed like hogs, and shot at like wild beasts."[108]

Slaves who tried to escape were often tortured without mercy. In the book *The Colored Patriots of the American Revolution,* William C. Nell describes a slave who ran away from a plantation and was recaptured by his owner, known only as Major Mitchell of the U.S. Army. The major burned the letter "M" into the slave's forehead to show that he was "Mitchell's slave." The slave described Mitchell in the dialect popular during the early eighteenth century when this story was told:

> Pious? I guess he was pious! . . . My last master—O, he biggest Christian! He 'pears pious. Ha! he big man—he tempt [to] shoot me 'cause I won't take off coat [for] him to whip me. Gun all ready [to] shoot me—I take off coat—he get rope, tie me to bang me—I kitched him, pulled him down, and ran away. Dat is de last of him I ever saw. . . . I want to get to Canada—dat's all I want. . . . I want to get out dis country.[109]

Words and Deeds in New England

Escaping was regarded as a serious crime, but it was even against the law for blacks to read or write in the southern colonies. A few slaves learned anyway, however, despite the fact that they could have been tortured or killed if discovered. In the North some blacks were educated by their owners, or at Quaker or Methodist schools. Phillis Wheatley was one such slave. She was kidnapped in Africa at the age of eight and purchased by Susannah Wheatley, a Boston woman who taught her young charge to read and write.

Phyllis Wheatley was a child prodigy, and began to write poems in 1773 at the age of thirteen. When they were first published, Wheatley's words touched a nerve in the colonies and were held up by abolitionists as proof that blacks should be educated and freed from bondage.

While Wheatley's poetic words inspired the reading public, the stirring words and actions of New England patriots encouraged some blacks to argue for their own liberty. As Rhode Island slave Jehu Grant wrote, "[When] I saw liberty poles and people all engaged for the support of freedom, I could not but like and be pleased with such thing."[110]

In Massachusetts, where the Revolution was born, slaves began petitioning courts for their freedom almost as soon as the Stamp Act controversy stirred calls for independence. In 1766 an unnamed black woman in Massachusetts sued for her freedom while John Adams looked on in the courtroom. In 1769 a Boston slave named John Swain convinced the Nantucket court to grant him his freedom. A slave named Caesar Henrick sued his master and was awarded monetary damages, according to an 1847 article in the Boston *Courier:*

> [In] October, 1773, an action was brought against Richard Greenleaf, of Newburyport, by Caesar [Henrick], a colored man, whom he claimed as his slave, for holding him in bondage. [Henrick] laid the damages at fifty pounds. . . . [The] jury brought in their verdict, and

awarded [Henrick] eighteen pounds, damages and costs.[111]

Several other slaves obtained their freedom this way, but it was a long, expensive, and difficult process, especially because the majority of blacks could not read or write. And since these were civil suits, they did not set any legal precedent such as freeing all slaves in Massachusetts.

In January 1773 a group of slaves including Peter Petion, Sambo Freeman, and Felix Holbrook tried to remedy this problem by petitioning the general court of the state legislature for their freedom. In an emotional plea, they wrote that their legal status as slaves deprived them of family and nation, saying, "We have no property! we have no wives! we have no children! no city! no country!"[112] When the legislature failed to act, the men went to the office of governor Tom Hutchinson, who claimed he could not help them. In May 1774 the group sent another petition to the legislature, but were again ignored. Six weeks later they again asked for their freedom and also for small parcels of land so that "each of us may there sit down quietly under his own fig tree."[113]

Although the petition was once again denied, by the end of the Revolution, slavery was virtually abolished through legislative process and court actions in Pennsylvania, Vermont, Massachusetts, Connecticut, Rhode Island, New York, and New Jersey.

The Petition for Freedom

On May 25, 1774, a group of black slaves sent a petition to the Massachusetts legislature asking for their freedom. The petition was reprinted with its original eighteenth-century spelling intact by Ray Raphael in *A People's History of the American Revolution*.

"The Petition of a Grate Number of Blackes of this Province who by divine permission are held in a state of Slavery with the bowels of a free and christian Country
   Humbly Shewing
   That your Petitioners apprehend we have in common with all other men a naturel right to our freedoms without Being depriv'd of them by our fellow men as we are a freeborn Pepel and have never forfeited this Blessing by [any] compact or agreement whatever. But we were unjustly dragged by the cruel hand of power from our dearest [friends] and sum of us stolen from the bosoms of our tender Parents and from a Populous Pleasant and plentiful country and Brought hither to be made slaves for Life in a Christian land.

   Thus we are deprived of every thing that hath a tendency to make life even tolerable, the endearing ties of husband and wife we are strangers to for we are no longer man and wife than our masters or mistresses thinkes proper marred or [unmarried]. Our children are also taken from us by force and sent [many] miles from us wear we seldom or ever see them again there to be made slave of for Life which sumtimes is [very] short by Reson of Being dragged from their mothers [breast]. Thus our Lives are imbittered to us on these accounts. . . .

   We therfor [beg] your Excellency and Honours will give this its deer weight and consideration and that you will accordingly cause an act of the legislative to be passed that we may obtain our Natural right our freedoms and our children be set at [liberty]."

Despite the loosening of slavery's bonds, blacks both free and slave continued to be abused by the public. A freeman named Prince Hall delivered a sermon to the African Masonic Lodge in Boston describing the difficulties experienced by the city's black population:

[Let] us pray God . . . would give us the grace of patience, and strength to bear up under all our troubles, which. . . we have our share of. Patience, I say; for were we not possessed of a great measure of it, we could not bear up under the daily insults we meet with in the streets of Boston. . . . How, at such times, are we shamefully abused, and that to such a degree, that we may truly be said to carry our lives in our hands, and the arrows of death are flying about our heads. Helpless women have their clothes torn from their backs . . . by a mob or horde of shameless, low-lived, envious, spiteful persons—some of them, not long since, servants in gentlemen's kitchens . . . horse-tenders, chaise-drivers. I was told by a gentleman who saw the filthy behavior in the Common, that, in all places he had been in, he never saw so cruel behavior in all his life. . . . Not only this man, but many in town, who have seen their behavior to us, and that, without provocation, twenty or thirty cowards have fallen upon one man. (O, the patience of the blacks!) [It] is not for want of courage in you, for they know that they do not face you man for man; but in a mob, which

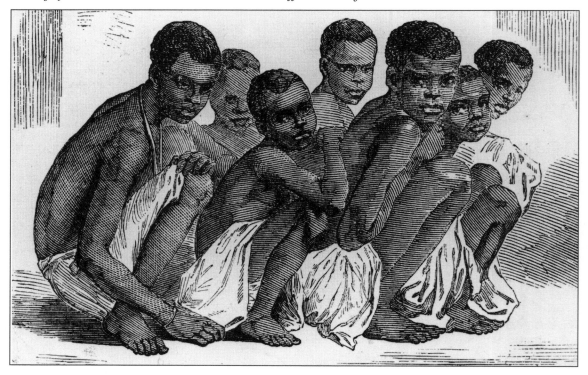

A group of young slaves. Although the courts and lawmakers virtually abolished slavery after the Revolution, blacks continued to suffer abuse by whites.

we despise, and would rather suffer wrong than to do wrong, to the disturbance of the community, and the disgrace of our reputation.[114]

"Mercy to Our Masters?"

While free blacks in the North faced their own problems, black slaves in the South were viewed with great suspicion by white slaveholders, who lived in constant fear that the threat of war might also inspire slave revolts. One widespread rumor was explained by Benjamin Quarles in *The Negro in the American Revolution:* "In . . . North Carolina the climate of fear was intensified by the widely held belief that the British had decreed that every Negro who put his master to death would come into possession of his master's plantation."[115]

The flames of fear were fanned by southern newspapers, as Thad W. Tate writes in *The Negro in Eighteenth-Century Williamsburg:* "Newspapers all over the colonies were quick to publish every available detail of a real or rumored attempt of slaves to rebel; and much of the restrictive legislation against Negroes . . . was admittedly aimed at this unwelcome possibility."[116]

In one such case the fears of insurrection were justified. In the late 1770s a wealthy South Carolina planter identified only as Mr. Duncan painted his face black and disguised himself in slave clothes in order to infiltrate a meeting held by slaves in a clearing in the woods. By torchlight, Duncan observed a tall man standing atop a tree stump addressing the crowd. The man initiated a debate over how the assembled slaves should react when the war began:

"And now, boys, if the British land here in Caroliny, what shall we do with our masters?" [Another man answered] exclaiming, with fierce gestures, "Ravish [their] wives and daughters before their eyes, as they have done to *us.* Hunt them with hounds, as they have hunted *us.* Shoot them down with rifles, as they have shot *us.* Throw their carcasses to the crows, they have fattened on *our* bones; and then let the Devil take them. . . . Who talks of mercy to our masters?"[117]

Despite such rhetoric there were only a few scattered insurrections before 1775. Slaves who were caught fomenting rebellion were treated harshly—whipped, mutilated, tortured, or hanged. Even so, the fear of slave rebellion was used to manipulate public opinion by both sides in the American Revolution.

Meanwhile the British actually did encourage slaves to run away from their plantations and join the loyalist cause under the false pretense that the English would treat the blacks better than their masters had done. This widely held view was demonstrated by a 1773 ad in the *Virginia Gazette* in which the owner of a missing couple stated that the pair might have escaped to Great Britain, "where they will be free (a Notion now too prevalent among the Negroes, greatly to the Vexation and Prejudice of their Masters)."[118]

In response to colonists' fears, the already repressive conditions for blacks were made even worse. Slaveholders organized posses to patrol country lanes at night. Slaves carrying weapons, gathered in groups, or caught out on the roads after nine o'clock were beaten or killed. In North Carolina the Committee of Safety, formed to fight the Revolution, issued these orders:

Resolved, that the Patrolers shoot one or any number of Negroes who are armed and doth not willingly surrender their arms, and that they have the Discretionary Power, to shoot to any Number of Negroes above four, who are off their Masters Plantations, and will not submitt.[119]

The result of such proclamations ensured that slaves who might have even whispered about escaping were suspected of conspiracy and subjected to imprisonment and merciless torture.

Dunmore's Ethiopian Regiment

Further confusion was added to the situation when, in November 1775, Lord Dunmore, the royal governor of Virginia, issued a proclamation freeing all indentured servants and blacks, and inviting them to join the British army in order to force the colonists to obey the will of King George III.

Dunmore's words inspired thousands of slaves to run away, some with their owners' guns, ammunition, and clothing. In two Virginia counties alone, two thousand slaves ran away within weeks of the proclamation. As rumor spread among slaves that more than forty thousand blacks had escaped to join the British, a song was passed from plantation to plantation that said:

> You may beat upon my body,
> But you cannot harm [my] soul;
> I shall join the forty thousand by and by.

> You may sell my children to Georgy [Georgia],

Fighting for the British

Early in the war escaped slaves fought heroically for the British cause, serving in Lord Dunmore's Ethiopian Regiment, as Benjamin Quarles explains in *The Negro in the American Revolution.*

"The first and only major military action in which Dunmore's forces engaged was the battle of Great Bridge. Of the Governor's troops of some six hundred men, nearly half were Negroes. Of the eighteen wounded prisoners taken by the Virginians in this rout, two were former slaves. One of them, James Anderson, was wounded 'in the Forearm—Bones shattered and flesh much torn.' The other one, Casar, was hit 'in the Thigh, by a [musket] Ball. . . .' After the fiasco at Great Bridge, the Governor was forced to operate from his ships. Taking aboard the hardiest of his Negro followers and placing them under officers who exercised them at small arms, he [confidently] awaited recruits.

Dunmore's use of Negroes also embraced maritime service. On the six [boats] sent by the Governor to cannonade Hampton in late October 1775, there were colored crewmen, two of whom were captured when the Virginians seized the pilot boat *Hawk Tender.* To man the small craft that scurried in and out of the river settlements, harassing the plantations, the British depended largely on ex-slaves, particularly as pilots. Joseph Harris, a runaway, served as pilot of the *Otter,* having come to Captain Matthew Squire with the highest recommendation from a fellow naval officer. 'I think him too useful to His Majesty's service to take away,' wrote the latter, because of 'his being well acquainted with many creeks in the Eastern Shore.'"

But you cannot harm their soul;
They will join the forty thousand by
and by.

Come, slave-trader, come in too;
The Lord's got a pardon here for you;
You shall join the forty thousand by
and by.[120]

Those inspired by Dunmore's proclamation escaped to British ships, and about three hundred men formed a black fighting force known as Lord Dunmore's Ethiopian Regiment. Their uniforms proudly displayed the inscription "Liberty to slaves" over their breasts.

Dunmore had high hopes for the regiment, but his plan was thwarted by a smallpox epidemic that swept through the black population, hitting hardest those who lived aboard overcrowded ships without warm clothing or sufficient food. The disappointed Dunmore wrote a letter to a friend, saying that his black regiment "would have been in great forwardness had not a fever crept in amongst them, which carried off a great many very fine fellows."[121]

Despite this tragedy slaves continued to run away, and by the end of the war, more than one hundred thousand enslaved people—nearly one in five—had joined the British cause. Thomas Jefferson calculated that in Virginia in 1778 alone, more than thirty thousand blacks defected to the loyalist side.

Black Patriots

When the war began a few hundred northern slaves emulated those in the South and defected to the loyalist side. Unlike Lord Dunmore, however, few northern governors were willing to recruit blacks into the military service, so a far smaller number escaped to the British side. Instead, possibly because of the small progress seen in the courts, most northern blacks sided with the patriot cause.

One of the most well-known black patriots was Crispus Attucks, a former slave from Massachusetts who died in the Boston Massacre. Attucks had been a free man since 1750, working on whaling ships to earn a living. While on shore leave in Boston in February 1770, the forty-six-year-old Attucks attended several demonstrations against the British who were then occupying the city. At one protest Attucks gave a brief speech about resisting the British and urged his fellow Americans to join together in resistance.

On March 5 Attucks led a group of about sixty men in a rowdy street demonstration on Boston's town square. They marched to the Customs House and began abusing the guard there with chunks of ice, snowballs, and rocks. A group of soldiers approached the scene. According to an eyewitness known only as Botta,

[A] band of the populace, led by a mulatto named ATTUCKS, . . . brandished their clubs, and pelted [the redcoats] with snowballs. The maledictions, the imprecations, the execrations of the multitude, were horrible. In the midst of a torrent of invective from every quarter, the military were challenged to fire. The populace advanced to the points of their bayonets. The soldiers appeared like statues; the cries, the howlings, the menaces, the violent din of bells still sounding the alarm, increased the confusion and the horrors of these moments; at length, the mulatto and twelve of his companions, pressing forward, environed the soldiers, and striking their muskets with their clubs, cried to the multitude: *"Be not afraid; they dare not fire: why do you hesitate, why do you not kill them, why not crush them at once?"* [Attucks]

Black patriot Crispus Attucks was killed during the Boston Massacre.

lifted his arm against Capt. Preston, and having turned one of the muskets, he seized the bayonet with his left hand, as if he intended to execute his threat. At this moment, confused cries were heard: *"The wretches dare not fire!"* Firing succeeds. ATTUCKS is slain. The other discharges follow. Three were killed, five severely wounded, and several others slightly.

ATTUCKS had formed the patriots in Dock Square, from whence they marched up King street, passing through the street up to the main guard, in order to make the attack. ATTUCKS . . . had been foremost in resisting, and was first slain. As proof of a front engagement, he received two [musket] balls, one in each breast.[122]

The Rhode Island Battalion

Years after the Boston Massacre, when the Revolution began in earnest, slaves and freemen joined colonial forces, and they were present at every battle from Lexington and Bunker Hill to Yorktown. Despite this fact, General Washington and other leaders were loath to let blacks join the Continental Army. As Quarles writes, "The negative attitude towards enlisting the [black] man sprang from a reluctance to deprive a master of his apprenticed servant or chattel slave, and from the fear of putting guns in the hands of a class of persons most of whom were not free."[123]

The severe shortage of manpower, however, motivated state legislatures to draft black men into the Revolutionary armies. And there were many African Americans eager to go to war for the promise of freedom. As a black Revolutionary War veteran known as Dr. Harris said in a speech in 1829,

> *Then* liberty *meant* something. Then, liberty, independence, freedom, were in every man's mouth. They were the sounds at which they rallied, and under which they fought and bled. They were the words which encouraged and cheered them through their hunger, and nakedness, and fatigue, in cold and in heat. The word slavery then filled their hearts with horror. They fought because they would not be slaves. Those whom liberty has cost nothing, do not know how to prize it.[124]

With thousands like Harris ready to join the cause, Massachusetts began drafting free blacks in 1777. In 1778 Rhode Island passed a law allowing slaves to join the Continental Army. And in a precedent-setting move, black soldiers would be freed and given compensation and benefits equal to those of white soldiers.

Records show that the all-black First Regiment served honorably and with great distinction from 1778 until the end of the war in 1783. At the battle at Red Bank, according to Nell,

> [The] blacks formed an entire regiment, and they discharged their duty with zeal and fidelity. The gallant defense of Red Bank . . . is among the proofs of their valor. In this contest, it will be recollected that four hundred men met and repulsed, after a terrible and sanguinary [bloody] struggle, fifteen hundred Hessian troops.[125]

With five years of uninterrupted service, the Rhode Island First stayed together longer than most white units that served in the Continental Army. They were present at many key battles, including Fort Oswego, New York, and the final British defeat at Yorktown. At the Battle of Rhode Island, in which Continental troops were forced to retreat, a white soldier described the behavior of the soldiers in the First Regiment: *Three times in succession* they were attacked, with most desperate valor and fury, by well disciplined and veteran troops, and three times did they successfully repel the assault, and thus preserve our army from capture. They fought through the war. They were brave, hearty troops."[126]

When the war finally ended, the black soldiers—like their white counterparts—were simply sent on their way with no compensation for their service. At the final address to the troops, white regiment commander Jeremiah Olney praised the soldiers' "unexampled fortitude and patience through all the dangers and toils in a long and severe war. . . . [He also declared] his [deep admiration] of their valor and good conduct displayed on every occasion when called to face an enemy in the field."[127]

Olney also expressed his profound regret that wages and back pay owed to the soldiers would likely never be received, although he promised to argue before Congress to settle the accounts of the men in the regiment. Then as Lorenzo J. Greene writes in *Slavery, Revolutionary America, and the New Nation,* "hungry, penniless, ragged, some of them sick or injured, [the black soldiers] began the hot, dusty march back to Rhode Island. There . . . [they] fought to restrain their erstwhile masters from reenslaving them. Gradually they lapsed into oblivion, forgotten by the ungrateful nation for which they had sacrificed so much to establish."[128]

Spies and Laborers

While northern colonies formed segregated black regiments, in the South blacks who served in the Continental Army fought side by side with white soldiers. Southern slaves were often enlisted in the army to fulfill the military duties of their white masters. Other blacks were simply purchased by the army as slaves and forced to work with no compensation. Whatever their background, southern blacks served in the army and the navy and even worked as spies.

A slave named Antigua from South Carolina was a noted spy who went behind British lines to gather information about troop movements. Saul Mathews, another slave, performed the same service in Virginia. Ten years after the end of the war, Mathews was granted his freedom by the state for his essential services in the Revolution. Blacks also acted as messengers, carrying military intelligence to generals stationed throughout the colonies.

Southern slaves also added to the war effort by building and maintaining hundreds of miles of roads, working with shovels, pickaxes, and hoes. They traveled the back roads destroying bridges, cutting down trees, and building forts to thwart enemy advances. In Maryland skilled black ironworkers labored at the cannon foundry at Antietam. In South Carolina, they worked as firemen. In Virginia the navy recruited slaves to act as carpenters, sawyers, tree-fallers, and blacksmiths. Slaves also worked in shipyards and military hospitals.

"Bravery and Fortitude"

While some blacks worked behind the scene, others served closer to the front lines. And although life was difficult for all soldiers serving in the Revolution, African Americans suffered special hardships. In the military, they were never promoted beyond the rank of private, and often remained nameless, carried on in the books as "A Negro Man," or "Negro by Name," or "A Negro name not known."[129]

Few blacks were allowed to fight on horseback in the cavalry, but some served with artillery regiments, operating the big guns. Most often, blacks served in the infantry. Barred from carrying guns, they acted as waiters, cooks, or personal attendants for officers.

Depite enduring daily prejudice many blacks served with honor and distinction. Edward Hector of Pennsylvania single-handedly defended an ammunition wagon from capture by the enemy. Fifty years after the battle he was awarded $40 by the state of Pennsylvania for his heroism. Austin Dabney of Georgia joined the military with his master and forty years later was awarded his freedom and 112 acres of land for "bravery and fortitude . . . in several engagements and actions [against the enemy]."[130] Many hundreds of black soldiers served courageously without such recorded compensation.

The American Revolution was a chaotic time when the conventions of society were torn asunder. British governors, mayors, and legislators were replaced by Americans. Blacks were caught in a political tug of war between the Americans and the British, and both sides seriously mistreated them.

African Americans, both slave and free, served in every battle and skirmish of the war under both British and American command. When the Revolution was over and white Americans were given their freedom and liberty, blacks discovered that the poetic words in the Declaration of Independence were not written for them. Those who had helped fight the war returned to their lowly status as chattel slaves or freemen trying to survive in a world of prejudice, discrimination, and worse.

Notes

Introduction: Seeds of Revolution

1. Hoag Levins, "Indian King Tavern Museum: The Revolutionary Era," 1995–2001. www.levins.com/ik7.html.
2. Thomas Paine, "Of the Present Ability of America, with Some Miscellaneous Reflexions," *Common Sense*. www.bartleby.com/133/index.html.
3. Ray Raphael, *A People's History of the American Revolution*. New York: New Press, 2001, p. 305.

Chapter 1: Farm and Village Life

4. Nathaniel Newcomer, *The Embattled Farmers*. New York: King's Crown Press, 1953, p. 2.
5. Oscar and Lilian Handlin, *A Restless People*. Garden City, NY: Anchor Press/Doubleday, 1982, p. 8.
6. Quoted in Evarts B. Greene, *The Revolutionary Generation: 1763–1790*. Chicago: Quadrangle Books, 1971, p. 26.
7. Handlin, *A Restless People*, p. 11.
8. Patrick M'Robert, *A Tour Through Part of the North Provinces of America*. New York: New York Times and Arno Press, 1968, p. 37.
9. M'Robert, *A Tour Through Part of the North Provinces of America*, p. 6.
10. Newcomer, *The Embattled Farmers*, p. 4.
11. Ann Hulton, *Letters of a Loyalist Lady*. Cambridge, MA: Harvard University Press, 1927, p. 105.
12. Quoted in Newcomer, *The Embattled Farmers*, p. 25.
13. Quoted in Newcomer, *The Embattled Farmers*, p. 33.
14. Quoted in Newcomer, *The Embattled Farmers*, p. 39.
15. Quoted in Raphael, *A People's History of the American Revolution*, p. 35.
16. Quoted in Newcomer, *The Embattled Farmers*, p. 41.
17. Daniel J. Boorstin, *The Americans: The Colonial Experience*. New York: Random House, 1958, p. 105.
18. Handlin, *A Restless People*, p. 18.
19. T.H. Breen, *Tobacco Culture*. Princeton, NJ: Princeton University Press, 1985, p. 41.
20. Quoted in Breen, *Tobacco Culture*, p. 32.
21. Mark Mastromarino, "Biography of George Washington," Papers of George Washington, 1999. www.virginia.edu/gwpapers/faq/washbio.html.
22. Breen, *Tobacco Culture*, p. 183.
23. Handlin, *A Restless People*, pp. 206–207.
24. Raphael, *A People's History of the American Revolution*, p. 76.
25. Quoted in Newcomer, *The Embattled Farmers*, p. 111.
26. Lydia Minturn Post, *Personal Recollections of the American Revolution*. Port Washington, NY: Kennikat Press, 1970, p. 26.
27. Post, *Personal Recollections of the American Revolution*, p. 34.

Chapter 2: City Life

28. Gary B. Nash, *The Urban Crucible: The Northern Seaports and the Origins of the American Revolution*. Cambridge, MA: Harvard University Press, 1986, p. 1.
29. Quoted in Dirk Hoerder, *Crowd Action in Revolutionary Massachusetts 1765–*

1780. New York: Academic Press, 1977, p. 97.

30. Quoted in Robert Blair St. George, ed., *Material Life in America 1600–1860.* Boston: Northeastern University Press, 1988, p. 239.

31. Quoted in Virginia Draper Harrington, *The New York Merchant on the Eve of the Revolution.* Gloucester, MA: P. Smith, 1964, p. 323.

32. Nash, *The Urban Crucible,* p. 156.

33. Quoted in Nash, *The Urban Crucible,* p. 161.

34. Quoted in Nash, *The Urban Crucible,* p. 205.

35. Hoerder, *Crowd Action in Revolutionary Massachusetts 1765–1780,* p. 98.

36. Nash, *The Urban Crucible,* p. 186.

37. Quoted in Raphael, *A People's History of the American Revolution,* p. 14.

38. Quoted in Nash, *The Urban Crucible,* p. 191.

39. Quoted in Kym S. Rice, *Early American Taverns: For the Entertainment of Friends and Strangers.* Chicago: Regnery Gateway, 1983, p. 122.

40. Quoted in Rice, *Early American Taverns,* p. 123.

41. Levins, "Indian King Tavern Museum: The Revolutionary Era."

42. Quoted in John C. Dann, ed., *The Revolution Remembered.* Chicago: University of Chicago Press, 1980, p. 4.

43. Donald Barr Chidsey, *The Siege of Boston.* New York: Crown, 1966, p. 102.

44. Quoted in Ray W. Pettengill, trans., *Letters from America: 1776–1779.* Port Washington, NY: Kennikat Press, 1964, p. 181.

45. Ewald Gustav Schaukirk, *Occupation of New York City by the British.* New York: New York Times and Arno Press, 1969, pp. 1–2.

46. Schaukirk, *Occupation of New York City by the British,* p. 3.

47. Schaukirk, *Occupation of New York City by the British,* p. 3.

48. Schaukirk, *Occupation of New York City by the British,* p. 10.

49. John W. Jackson, *With the British Army in Philadelphia 1777–1778.* San Rafael, CA: Presidio Press, 1979, p. 90.

50. Quoted in Pettengill, *Letters from America,* pp. 182–83.

51. Quoted in Pettengill, *Letters from America,* p. 184.

52. "Personalities," Intelligence in the War of Independence, n.d. www.odci.gov/cia /publications/warindep/frames.html.

53. Jackson, *With the British Army in Philadelphia 1777–1778,* pp. 265–66.

54. Raphael, *A People's History of the American Revolution,* p. 302.

Chapter 3: Lives of Revolutionary Soldiers

55. Harold L. Peterson, *The Book of the Continental Soldier.* Harrisburg, PA: Stackpole, 1968, p. 16.

56. Roger Lamb, *An Original and Authentic Journal of Occurrences During the Late American War.* New York: New York Times and Arno Press, 1968, pp. 23–24.

57. Joseph Plumb Martin, *Adventures of a Revolutionary Soldier.* Ed. George F. Scheer. Boston: Little, Brown, 1962, p. 6.

58. Quoted in Raphael, *A People's History of the American Revolution,* p. 48.

59. Lamb, *An Original and Authentic Journal of Occurrences During the Late American War,* p. 26.

60. Quoted in Raphael, *A People's History of the American Revolution,* p. 49.

61. Quoted in Raphael, *A People's History of the American Revolution,* p. 54.

62. Quoted in Margaret Wheeler Willard, ed., *Letters on the American Revolution: 1774–1776.* Port Washington, NY: Kennikat Press, 1968, p. 349.

63. Quoted in Dann, *The Revolution Remembered,* p. 106.

64. Quoted in Raphael, *A People's History of the American Revolution,* p. 54.

65. Quoted in Milton Meltzer, *The American Revolutionaries: A History in Their Own Words 1750–1800.* New York: Thomas Y. Crowell, 1987, p. 61.

66. Quoted in Dann, *The Revolution Remembered,* p. 132.

67. Alexander Graydon, *Memoirs of a Life, Chiefly Passed in Pennsylvania.* Harrisburg, PA: J. Wyeth, 1811, p. 135.

68. Quoted in Dann, *The Revolution Remembered,* p. 17.

69. Quoted in Dann, *The Revolution Remembered,* p. 55.

70. Quoted in Sara Bertha Townsend, *An American Soldier: The Life of John Laurens.* Raleigh, NC: Edwards & Broughton, 1958, p. 63.

71. Peterson, *The Book of the Continental Soldier,* p. 114.

72. Quoted in Dann, *The Revolution Remembered,* p. 132.

73. Martin, *Adventures of a Revolutionary Soldier,* pp. 51–52.

74. Martin, *Adventures of a Revolutionary Soldier,* p. 41.

75. Quoted in Dann, *The Revolution Remembered,* pp. 156–57.

76. Martin, *Adventures of a Revolutionary Soldier,* p. 89.

77. Quoted in Charles Knowles Bolton, *The Private Soldier Under Washington.* Port Washington, NY: Kennikat Press, 1964, pp. 51–52.

78. Martin, *Adventures of a Revolutionary Soldier,* pp. 102–103.

Chapter 4: Women in the Revolution

79. Joan R. Gundersen, *To Be Useful to the World.* New York: Twayne, 1996, p. 4.

80. Lonnelle Aikman, "Patriots in Petticoats," *National Geographic,* October 1975, pp. 475–76.

81. Gundersen, *To Be Useful to the World,* p. 22.

82. Gundersen, *To Be Useful to the World,* p. 70.

83. Raphael, *A People's History of the American Revolution,* p. 108.

84. Quoted in Raphael, *A People's History of the American Revolution,* p. 111.

85. Eliza Wilkinson, *Letters of Eliza Wilkinson.* Ed. Caroline Gilman. New York: New York Times and Arno Press, 1969, p. 17.

86. Post, *Personal Recollections of the American Revolution,* p. 75.

87. Post, *Personal Recollections of the American Revolution,* p. 166.

88. Post, *Personal Recollections of the American Revolution,* p. 85.

89. Wilkinson, *Letters of Eliza Wilkinson,* p. 28.

90. Wilkinson, *Letters of Eliza Wilkinson,* pp. 30–31, p. 46.

91. Post, *Personal Recollections of the American Revolution*, pp. 93–94.

92. Quoted in Linda K. Kerber, *Women of the Republic: Intellect and Ideology in Revolutionary America*. Chapel Hill: University of North Carolina Press, 1980, p. 44.

93. Aikman, "Patriots in Petticoats," p. 477.

94. Quoted in Kerber, *Women of the Republic*, p. 43.

95. Aikman, "Patriots in Petticoats," 479–80.

96. Quoted in Walter Hart Blumenthal, *Women Camp Followers of the American Revolution*. New York: Arno Press, 1974, p. 64.

97. Quoted in Blumenthal, *Women Camp Followers of the American Revolution*, p. 74.

98. Quoted in Blumenthal, *Women Camp Followers of the American Revolution*, p. 16.

99. Blumenthal, *Women Camp Followers of the American Revolution*, p. 19.

100. Quoted in Raphael, *A People's History of the American Revolution*, p. 124.

101. Quoted in Raphael, *A People's History of the American Revolution*, p. 115.

102. Wilkinson, *Letters of Eliza Wilkinson*, pp. 60–61.

103. Quoted in Aikman, "Patriots in Petticoats," p. 475.

Chapter 5: Black Americans, Free and Slave

104. Quoted in James Schouler, *Americans of 1776: Daily Life in Revolutionary America*. Williamstown, MA: Corner House, 1976, p. 14.

105. Post, *Personal Recollections of the American Revolution*, pp. 47–48.

106. Quoted in Winthrop D. Jordan, *White Over Black*. Baltimore, MD: Penguin Books, 1968, p. 274.

107. South Carolina Information Highway, "The Lives of African-American Slaves in Carolina During the 18th Century," 1998–2000. www.sciway.net/hist/chicora/slavery18-3.html.

108. Quoted in William C. Nell, *The Colored Patriots of the American Revolution*. New York: Arno Press, 1968, p. 248.

109. Quoted in Nell, *The Colored Patriots of the American Revolution*, p. 222.

110. Quoted in Dann, *The Revolution Remembered*, p. 28.

111. Quoted in Nell, *The Colored Patriots of the American Revolution*, p. 44.

112. Quoted in Benjamin Quarles, *The Negro in the American Revolution*. Chapel Hill: University of North Carolina Press, 1966, p. 39.

113. Quoted in Raphael, *A People's History of the American Revolution*, p. 293.

114. Quoted in Nell, *The Colored Patriots of the American Revolution*, pp. 62–63.

115. Quarles, *The Negro in the American Revolution*, p. 14.

116. Thad W. Tate, *The Negro in Eighteenth-Century Williamsburg*. Charlottesville: University Press of Virginia, 1965, pp. 201–202.

117. Quoted in Nell, *The Colored Patriots of the American Revolution*, p. 248.

118. Quoted in Raphael, *A People's History of the American Revolution*, p. 247.

119. Quoted in Raphael, *A People's History of the American Revolution*, p. 248.

120. Quoted in Nell, *The Colored Patriots of the American Revolution*, p. 249.

121. Quoted in Quarles, *The Negro in the American Revolution*, p. 30.

122. Quoted in Nell, *The Colored Patriots of the American Revolution*, pp. 16–17.

123. Quarles, *The Negro in the American Revolution,* p. xxvii.
124. Quoted in Nell, *The Colored Patriots of the American Revolution,* p. 129.
125. Nell, *The Colored Patriots of the American Revolution,* p. 126.
126. Quoted in Raphael, *A People's History of the American Revolution,* p. 287.
127. Quoted in Paul Finkelman, ed., *Slavery, Revolutionary America, and the New Nation.* New York: Garland, 1989, p. 243.
128. Quoted in Finkelman, *Slavery, Revolutionary Amer- ica, and the New Nation,* p. 244.
129. Quoted in Quarles, *The Negro in the American Revolution,* p. 74.
130. Quoted in Quarles, *The Negro in the American Revolution,* p. 75.

For Further Reading

Ruth Dean and Melissa Thomson, *Life in the American Colonies*. San Diego: Lucent Books, 1999. Discusses the day-to-day life of country and city people in the American colonies, including members of different professions and slaves.

Mary R. Furbee, *Women of the American Revolution*. San Diego: Lucent Books, 1999. Chronicles the contributions of various women who helped the American colonies break free of British rule, including Abigail Adams, Mercy Warren, and others.

Judith E. Harper, *African Americans and the Revolutionary War*. Chanhassen, MN: Child's World, 2001. Examines the hardships suffered by African Americans and their contributions during the Revolutionary War.

Daniel C. Littlefield, *Revolutionary Citizens: African Americans, 1776–1804*. New York: Oxford University Press, 1997. Discusses the lives of African Americans during the Revolutionary War and the years following.

Bonnie L. Lukes, *The American Revolution*. San Diego: Lucent Books, 1996. A detailed account of the events leading up to the Revolution, the war, and the aftermath.

Joseph Plumb Martin, *Yankee Doodle Boy: A Young Soldier's Adventures in the American Revolution*. Ed. George F. Scheer. New York: Holiday House, 1995. A young adult version of Martin's fascinating account of his years as a soldier in the Continental Army between 1776 and 1783.

Harold L. Peterson, *The Book of the Continental Soldier*. Harrisburg, PA: Stackpole, 1968. Photos, illustrations, and text detail the uniforms, weapons, and equipment used by the Continental soldier.

Fran Zell, *A Multicultural Portrait of the American Revolution*. Tarrytown, NY: Benchmark Books, 1996. Describes the lives of Native Americans, African Americans, women, and others during the Revolutionary War era.

Works Consulted

Books

Wilber C. Abbott, *New York in the American Revolution.* Port Washington, NY: Ira J. Friedman, 1962. The history of New York City between 1763 and 1783 written by a professor of history at Harvard and originally published in 1929.

Walter Hart Blumenthal, *Women Camp Followers of the American Revolution.* New York: Arno Press, 1974. A well-researched book about women, known as camp followers, who followed Revolutionary armies from battle to battle, cooking, caring for the wounded, and sacrificing their personal well-being.

Charles Knowles Bolton, *The Private Soldier Under Washington.* Port Washington, NY: Kennikat Press, 1964. A thorough exploration of the average soldier's life under the command of George Washington during the Revolutionary War.

Daniel J. Boorstin, *The Americans: The Colonial Experience.* New York: Random House, 1958. A comprehensive history of colonial America exploring religion, agriculture, medicine, science, language, and culture by a professor of American history at the University of Chicago.

Patricia Bradley, *Slavery, Propaganda, and the American Revolution.* Jackson: University Press of Mississippi, 1998. An analysis of articles written by patriots before and during the American Revolution and how they deliberately avoided or distorted the harsh realities of slavery even as they argued for freedom and liberty for white Americans.

T.H. Breen, *Tobacco Culture.* Princeton, NJ: Princeton University Press, 1985. A thorough examination of the culture of the Chesapeake Bay tobacco planters on the eve of the American Revolution.

Carl Bridenbaugh, *Cities in Revolt: Urban Life in America, 1743–1776.* New York: Alfred A. Knopf, 1955. An in-depth look at city life in colonial America in the years before the Revolution, touching on urban culture, benefits, and problems.

Donald Barr Chidsey, *The Siege of Boston.* New York: Crown, 1966. An account of the beginning of the Revolution written as if the twentieth-century author was an eyewitness to the event.

John C. Dann, ed., *The Revolution Remembered.* Chicago: University of Chicago Press, 1980. A compilation of eyewitness accounts of the Revolution, written mostly by soldiers.

Thomas Dring and Albert G. Greene, *Recollections of the Jersey Prison Ship.* New York: Corinth Books, 1961. The memoirs of a navy captain about his appalling confinement on one of the most notorious prison ships of the Revolutionary War, first published in 1829.

Johann Ewald, Johann Hinrichs, and Johann Christoph von Huyn, *The Siege of Charleston.* Trans. and ed. Bernard A. Uhlendorf. New York: New York Times and Arno Press, 1968. An eyewitness account of the siege and capture of Charleston, South Carolina, written by Hessian soldiers who aided the British in this victory.

Paul Finkelman, ed., *Slavery, Revolutionary America, and the New Nation.* New York:

Garland, 1989. Several dozen articles written by leading historians about black participation in the Revolutionary War.

Alexander Graydon, *Memoirs of a Life, Chiefly Passed in Pennsylvania*. Harrisburg, PA: J. Wyeth, 1811. The reminiscences of a captain and his participation in the Revolutionary War.

Barbara Graymont, *The Iroquois in the American Revolution*. NY: Syracuse University Press, 1972. An examination of the role that the five tribes of the Iroquois played in the Revolution.

Evarts B. Greene, *The Revolutionary Generation: 1763–1790*. Chicago: Quadrangle Books, 1971. Examines the lives of the colonists before, during, and after the American Revolution, exploring the unique circumstances that allowed these very conservative people to rebel against their British rulers.

Joan R. Gundersen, *To Be Useful to the World*. New York: Twayne, 1996. A detailed and well-researched account of the lives of colonial women between 1740 and 1790.

Oscar and Lilian Handlin, *A Restless People*. Garden City, NY: Anchor Press/Doubleday, 1982. The way Americans lived in urban and rural areas between the years 1770 and 1778, written by a Harvard professor and his wife.

Virginia Draper Harrington, *The New York Merchant on the Eve of the Revolution*. Gloucester, MA: P. Smith, 1964. The economics, commerce, and history of pre-Revolution New York City.

Dirk Hoerder, *Crowd Action in Revolutionary Massachusetts 1765–1780*. New York: Academic Press, 1977. A study of demonstrations and political actions by large crowds in Massachusetts during the years of protest and war.

Ann Hulton, *Letters of a Loyalist Lady*. Cambridge, MA: Harvard University Press, 1927. The letters written in the 1770s by a British loyalist and sister of Henry Hulton, the commissioner of customs in Boston.

John W. Jackson, *With the British Army in Philadelphia 1777–1778*. San Rafael, CA: Presidio Press, 1979. A detailed history of the British occupation of Philadelphia during nineteen months of the Revolutionary War.

Winthrop D. Jordan, *White Over Black*. Baltimore, MD: Penguin Books, 1968. An exploration of white attitudes toward blacks from the first English explorations of Africa in the sixteenth century to the slavery in the United States in the early nineteenth century.

Linda K. Kerber, *Women of the Republic: Intellect and Ideology in Revolutionary America*. Chapel Hill: University of North Carolina Press, 1980. A study of the American Revolution through the eyes of women who worked in army hospitals and kitchens; acted as authors, spies, and fundraisers; fought in militias, and provided major support for the cause.

Roger Lamb, *An Original and Authentic Journal of Occurrences During the Late American War*. New York: New York Times and Arno Press, 1968. An eyewitness account of the American Revolution written in 1809 by a Welsh soldier serving under British command.

Joseph Plumb Martin, *Adventures of a Revolutionary Soldier*. Ed. George F. Scheer. Boston: Little, Brown, 1962. One of the few eyewitness accounts by an enlisted man; the author served in the Continental Army in New York, Pennsylvania, New Jersey, and elsewhere. First published in 1830, this book of battles, suffering, and woe has been a source for many books about the Revolution.

Milton Meltzer, *The American Revolutionaries: A History in Their Own Words 1750–1800*. New York: Thomas Y. Crowell, 1987. Letters, diaries, memoirs, and other written records of those who lived through the war for independence.

Lewis Henry Morgan, *League of the Ho-de-no-sau-nee or Iroquois*. New York: Citadel Press, 1993. Very detailed explanations of Iroquois daily life and traditions as seen through the eyes of a white American. First published in 1851, this book was one of the few written in the nineteenth century that treated Native Americans respectfully.

Richard B. Morris, *The Making of a Nation.* Vol. 2: 1775–1789. New York: Time, 1963. A riveting exploration of the American Revolution told with interesting facts, color paintings, and maps.

Patrick M'Robert, *A Tour through Part of the North Provinces of America.* New York: New York Times and Arno Press, 1968. The pithy observations of a Scotsman as he toured New York, New Jersey, Canada, and elsewhere in the year before the first shots of the Revolution were fired at Lexington.

Gary B. Nash, *The Urban Crucible: The Northern Seaports and the Origins of the American Revolution.* Cambridge, MA: Harvard University Press, 1986. A detailed explanation of the daily life, religion, and politics in the cities of the northern colonies and how these matters led to the Revolution.

William C. Nell, *The Colored Patriots of the American Revolution.* New York: Arno Press, 1968. A book first published in 1855 in which the author uses government documents, old newspaper articles, and interviews with elderly slaves to establish the fact that African Americans played an important part in the Revolution.

Nathaniel Newcomer, *The Embattled Farmers.* New York: King's Crown Press, 1953. The story of the Massachusetts countryside and how it was affected by the American Revolution.

Ray W. Pettengill, trans., *Letters from America: 1776–1779.* Port Washington, NY: Kennikat Press, 1964. The correspondence of British and Hessian officers to loved ones back home during the Revolution.

Lydia Minturn Post, *Personal Recollections of the American Revolution.* Port Washington, NY: Kennikat Press, 1970. The letters of a New York woman, first published in 1859, describing daily life during the British occupation.

Benjamin Quarles, *The Negro in the American Revolution.* Chapel Hill: University of North Carolina Press, 1966. The definitive book about blacks and their role in the American Revolution first published in 1961 by the professor emeritus of history at Morgan State University in Baltimore.

Ray Raphael, *A People's History of the American Revolution.* New York: New Press, 2001. A provocative and highly entertaining telling of the Revolution through the eyes of "real people," including working-class rebels, women, pacifists, Native Americans, and others, based on diaries, personal letters, and other eyewitness accounts.

Kym S. Rice, *Early American Taverns: For the Entertainment of Friends and Strangers.* Chicago: Regnery Gateway, 1983. A book about seventeenth- and eighteenth-century tavern keeping, entertainment, and management published for an exhibition at the Fraunces Tavern Museum in New York City, the site of George Washington's 1783 farewell address.

Ewald Gustav Schaukirk, *Occupation of New York City by the British.* New York: New York Times and Arno Press, 1969. Excerpts from the diary of a Prussian Moravian pastor as he recorded the scenes of the British occupation between 1775 and 1783.

James Schouler, *Americans of 1776: Daily Life in Revolutionary America.* Williamstown, MA: Corner House, 1976. A view of eighteenth-century American manners, morals, dress, and government from the perspective of the British author.

John Ferdinand Dalziel Smyth, *A Tour in the United States of America.* New York: New York Times, 1968. An eyewitness account of life in America during and immediately after the Revolution, first published in 1784.

Robert Blair St. George, ed., *Material Life in America 1600–1860.* Boston: Northeastern University Press, 1988. A study of American culture during the early years of the country written by various scholars in the fields of history, geography, art, and folklore.

Thad W. Tate, *The Negro in Eighteenth-Century Williamsburg.* Charlottesville: University Press of Virginia, 1965. A scholarly study of slavery in Williamsburg covering the growth of slavery, the slave population, jobs performed by Virginia slaves, slave auctions, black social life, and other topics.

Sara Bertha Townsend, *An American Soldier: The Life of John Laurens.* Raleigh, NC: Edwards & Broughton, 1958. The story of a South Carolina patriot and soldier as told by the correspondence between John Laurens and his father.

George M. Waller, *The American Revolution in the West.* Chicago: Nelson-Hall, 1976. A thorough exploration of the American Revolution on the western frontier.

George Washington, *The Writings Of George Washington from the Original Manuscript Sources, 1745–1799.* Ed. John C. Fitzpatrick. Washington, DC: 1931–1944. United States Government Printing Office. Hundreds of letters written by commander-in-chief of the Continental Army and the first president of the United States.

Eliza Wilkinson, *Letters of Eliza Wilkinson.* Ed. Caroline Gilman. New York: New York Times and Arno Press, 1969. One woman's view of the Revolution during the invasion and occupation of Charleston by the British, taken from a diary written by a young widow and first published in 1839.

Margaret Wheeler Willard, ed., *Letters on the American Revolution: 1774–1776.* Port Washington, NY: Kennikat Press, 1968. Correspondence from patriots, loyalists, politicians, soldiers, and wives concerning the early years of the war effort, first published in 1925.

Mike Wright, *What They* Didn't *Teach You About the American Revolution.* Novato,

CA: Presidio Press, 1999. A compilation of little-known facts about the American Revolution that are generally overlooked in history classes.

Internet Sources

David Cody, "Puritanism in New England," 1994. http://landow.stg.brown.edu/victorian/religion/puritan2.html. A website about the Puritans written by a winner of a Fulbright scholarship to Japan and associate professor of English at Hartwick College.

George Hewes, "Boston Tea Party—Eyewitness Account," The History Place American Revolution, www. historyplace.com/UnitedStates/revolution/teaparty.htm. A description of the famous tea party as told by a participant.

Independence Hall Association, "Betsy Ross: Her Life," 1996–2000. www.ushistory. org/betsy/ flaglife.html. A site dedicated to the woman who sewed the first American flag, with information about her life and work, along with flag rules, regulations, and trivia.

Thomas Jefferson, "Thomas Jefferson on Politics and Government," 1997–1999. http://etext.lib.virginia.edu/jefferson/quotations/jeffcont.htm. A collection of more than twenty-seven thousand quotations from the writings of Thomas Jefferson, which can be searched by category or keyword.

Hoag Levins, "Indian King Tavern Museum: The Revolutionary Era," 1995–2001. www. levins.com/ik7.html. A website maintained by the Indian King Tavern in Haddonfield, one of New Jersey's most historic buildings. Constructed in 1750, this is the tavern where the New Jersey constitution was written in 1777.

Mark Mastromarino, "Biography of George Washington," Papers of George Washington, 1999. www.virginia.edu/gwpapers/faq/washbio.html. A site with a detailed biography of America's first president, with links to important papers written by Washington, including his presidential farewell address and his thoughts on the Revolution.

J.D. Miller "Military History Online—Lexington and Concord," 2001. www. militaryhistoryonline.com/revolutionary/lexing tonconcord.asp. Details one of the most famous battles of the Revolutionary War.

Thomas Paine, "Of the Present Ability of America, with Some Miscellaneous Reflexions," Common Sense. www. bartleby.com/133/index.html. This site contains a reproduction of Thomas Paine's 1776 revolutionary tract Common Sense.

"Personalities," Intelligence in the War of Independence, n.d. www.odci.gov/cia/publications/warindep/frames.html. A publication of the Central Intelligence Agency that details intelligence, or spy, operations during the war, techniques used, and people involved.

Royal Proclamation of October 7, 1763, Bloorstreet.com. www.bloorstreet.com/200block/rp1763.htm. A website run by a Canadian law firm with legal documents and other links.

South Carolina Information Highway, "The Lives of African-American Slaves in Carolina During the 18th Century," 1998–2000. www.sciway.net/hist/chicora/slavery18-3.html. A site dedicated to "preserving the archaeological, historical, and cultural resources of the Carolinas" operated by the Chicora Foundation.

Wilcomb E. Washburn, "Indians and the American Revolution," n.d. http://americanrevolution.org/ind1.html. A website run by *AmericanRevolution.org.* that features articles from various respected historians on different aspects, viewpoints, and minutiae of the Revolution.

Barbara A. Wilson, "Women Soldiers in the American Revolutionary War," 1996–2000. http://userpages.aug.com/captbarb/femvets.html. Information about women who fought in American wars, including the Revolution, World Wars I and II, Vietnam, Desert Storm, and Bosnia, written by a retired captain in the U.S. air force.

Periodical

Lonnelle Aikman, "Patriots in Petticoats," *National Geographic,* October 1975. Details about women who played an integral part in the Revolution.

Index

Picture Credits

Cover photo: © Bettmann/CORBIS
© Bettmann/CORBIS, 24, 26, 30, 38, 64, 65, 90
© CORBIS, 79, 81, 82, 83
M. Diderot's Encyclopedia, 34, 67
The American Revolution, Picture Source Book by John Grafton, 13
Hulton/Archive by Getty Images, 32, 39, 41, 45, 47, 50, 53, 61, 66, 71, 72, 73, 86
I.N. Phelps Stokes Collection, 49
Library of Congress, 11, 14, 19, 21, 22, 23, 27, 31, 37, 52, 57, 76
National Archives, 12
Smithsonian Institution, 17
© Lee Snider/CORBIS, 16

About the Author

Stuart A. Kallen is the author of more than 150 nonfiction books for children and young adults. He has written on topics ranging from the theory of relativity to rock-and-roll history to life on the American frontier. In addition, Mr. Kallen has written award-winning children's videos and television scripts. In his spare time Stuart A. Kallen is a singer/songwriter/guitarist in San Diego, California.